Real Foodies'

슈퍼마켓 가자!

Korean
Supermarket
Food Stories

By Yeonsil Yoo

Hello 안녕하세요! 🐱

These days, Korean food is easier to find than ever. You don't even have to step into a specialty market—kimchi, instant noodles, and snacks are popping up in grocery aisles all over the world.

But if you're new to Korean food, it's not always clear where to start—or which brands are actually worth trying. And even if you already have your favorites, you might still wonder: How did these products get so popular? (Spoiler: They didn't just survive—they fought for their place, and along the way, became part of daily life in Korea.)

In this book, we'll explore some of Korea's most beloved snacks, noodles, and drinks—many of which you can now find at your local supermarket or Asian grocery. You'll get the story behind each one: how it began, how it won people over, and why it still matters today. Some are nostalgic comfort foods. Others went viral. A few even helped shape a generation. But all of them offer a glimpse into modern Korean culture.

You don't need to be a Korean food expert—just bring your curiosity and your appetite. Let's dig in!

Yeonsil Yoo

A Few Things to Know First

Korea / South Korea

Throughout this book, you'll see both "Korea" and "South Korea" used interchangeably. Unless otherwise noted, all mentions of "Korea" refer to South Korea—not North Korea.

Ramen / Ramyun / Ramyeon

These are all different English spellings of ramyeon (라면), the Korean word for instant noodles—pronounced somewhere between rah-myun and rah-myon. Different brands use different spellings (like "ramyun" or "ramen") for marketing purposes. In this book, I've followed each brand's official English name as sold in North America. Just a heads-up: brand names and spellings may change over time.

Snacks

In English, "snack" is a catch-all term for anything eaten between meals—fruit, nuts, yogurt, even leftovers. In Korean, though, gwaja (과자) is more specific. It refers only to packaged, shelf-stable snacks like chips, crackers, cookies, and puffs—not candy, chocolate, or baked goods like bread or pastries.

There's no perfect English equivalent for gwaja, so it's usually translated as "snack," even though the meanings don't fully align.

Content

1
The Staple Koreans Can't Live Without
Instant Noodle

2
Crunchy, Chewy, and Totally Addictive
Snacks

Sweet, Cold, and Uniquely Korean

Frozen Treats

Cool, Refreshing, and a Daily Pick-Me-Up

Drinks

Part 1

Instant Noodle

The Staple Koreans Can't Live Without

Samyang Ramen 삼양라면

Korea's First Instant Noodle

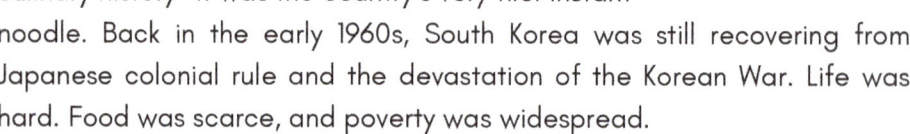

Samyang Ramen holds a special place in Korean culinary history—it was the country's very first instant noodle. Back in the early 1960s, South Korea was still recovering from Japanese colonial rule and the devastation of the Korean War. Life was hard. Food was scarce, and poverty was widespread.

Enter Jeon Joong-Yoon, the founder of Samyang Foods. He came from a well-off family, but one moment changed everything. He saw a long line of people waiting for watery porridge made from food scraps—a makeshift "meal" born out of desperation. The scene stayed with him. He felt called to do something about the hunger so many Koreans were facing.

People eating makeshift porridge made from food trash in the 1950s

Around that time, Japan had started to address its own food shortages. In 1958, Momofuku Ando introduced the world's first instant ramen: Chicken Ramen. Inspired, Jeon imported a few noodle-making machines from Japan. By 1963, *Samyang Ramen* was officially in production.

Early Samyang Ramen production site

Samyang Ramen launch ad featuring the headline:
"Today's Hot Topic! Our Food Challenges Are Solved"

The goal was simple: offer an affordable, filling meal to help ease the country's food crisis. *Samyang Ramen* launched at a very low price, making it accessible to almost everyone. But at first, people were hesitant. Wheat noodles weren't familiar—rice had always been the staple. So Samyang hit the streets, offering free tastings at movie theaters and public parks, hoping people would give it a try.

Then came a turning point. In the late 1960s, the Korean government began promoting non-rice alternatives to fight food shortages. And *Samyang Ramen*—cheap, quick, and satisfying—fit the bill perfectly. Sales soared. Before long, it had become a pantry staple across the country.

An ad with the slogan,
"Ramen is the second rice"

A Taste Adapted for Koreans

The first *Samyang Ramen* was modeled after Japan's Chicken Ramen, complete with a chicken on the package to highlight its flavor.

Japan's Chicken Ramen - the world's first instant ramen

Early Samyang Ramen emphasizing chicken flavor

But here's the thing—Korean taste preferences leaned more toward beef-based broths than chicken. So Samyang gradually adapted the flavor, shifting toward a richer, beefy broth. The inspiration? *Budae Jjigae* (Army Stew), a Korean comfort food born out of post-war necessity.

Budae Jjigae 부대찌개
(Army Stew)

During the Korean War, food was hard to come by. Near U.S. military bases, a small restaurant owner began using leftover army supplies—Spam, canned beans, cheese, sausages—to create hearty stews. Even though those ingredients are easy to find today, *budae jjigae* still stirs nostalgia and comfort for many Koreans.

Fast forward, and Samyang's flavor profile has come to reflect that same rich, savory essence—beef, ham, a touch of bone marrow—blended into a smooth, satisfying broth. With its chewy noodles and deep, savory flavor, *Samyang Ramen* remains one of Korea's top-selling instant noodles.

How to Make Army Stew with Samyang Ramen

1. Slice Spam, sausage, tofu, kimchi, and green onion to your liking.
2. Boil water (per package instructions).
3. Once boiling, add the noodles, soup powder, and all ingredients from Step 1 except green onion. Add a spoonful of canned beans.
4. When the noodles are cooked, add green onion, place a slice of cheese on top, and turn off the heat.
5. Serve hot and enjoy the spicy, umami-packed Budae Jjigae!

The Story Behind Korea's Favorite Comfort Food

Back in the 1950s, South Korea was in rough shape. After decades under Japanese colonial rule and the devastation of the Korean War, it was one of the poorest countries in the world—its GDP was less than half that of countries like Ghana and the Congo.

As part of postwar recovery efforts, the U.S. established military bases throughout Korea, including one in a city called *Uijeongbu*.

©NARA, Ohmynews.com

Local suppliers worked with these bases and noticed something surprising: large amounts of perfectly good food—ham, sausages, canned goods, and other processed meats—were being thrown away. Meanwhile, many Koreans were starving.

That's when the owner of a small food stall in Uijeongbu, *Odeng Sikdang*, quietly began purchasing those leftover ingredients from the nearby base. She stir-fried them with kimchi and gochugaru (Korean chili powder), creating a spicy, hearty stew that was cheap, filling, and—most importantly—delicious.

Odeng Sikdang

There was just one problem: selling food made with U.S. military surplus was illegal. So instead of calling it *budae jjigae* (which literally means "army base stew"), they gave it a more discreet name—*Myeongmul Jjigae* (명물찌개), meaning "the famous stew."

As Korea recovered and everyday ingredients became widely available, *budae jjigae* evolved. Today, it's no longer a dish of scraps—it's a full-on comfort food packed with instant noodles, glass noodles, Spam, sausage, tofu, baked beans, and cheese, all simmered in a rich, spicy beef bone broth. It's a symbol of resilience, reinvention, and finding flavor even in the hardest times.

Yukgaejang Sabalmyun 육개장 사발면

Korea's All-Time Best-Selling Cup Noodle

If you ask any Korean about their go-to cup noodle, they'd probably say *Yukgaejang Sabalmyun*. First introduced in 1982, it quickly became a household staple—and it's held the #1 spot in Korea's cup noodle category ever since.

Korean Market Version

International Market Version

The international version is adjusted to be less spicy.

Spicy Beef Stew (Yukgaejang) 육개장

The name *Yukgaejang* comes from a traditional spicy Korean beef stew, while *Sabalmyun* means "bowl noodle." But this instant version isn't an exact replica of the dish. Instead, it offers its own take: a soy-sauce-based beef broth that's mildly spicy with a subtle sweetness.

What sets it apart is the noodles. They're thin, springy, and cook quickly—soaking up the broth's deep, comforting flavor with just the right bite.

Over the years, Nongshim (the company behind *Yukgaejang Sabalmyun*) tried launching larger cup versions and even a pack-style format. But none of them took off. The original small cup remains the timeless favorite.

A Latecomer's Advantage

Interestingly, *Yukgaejang Sabalmyun* wasn't Korea's first cup noodle. That title goes to Samyang's *Cup Ramyun*, introduced in 1972 and modeled after Japan's *Nissin Cup Noodle*.

But the thing is, cup noodle packaging was quite expensive at the time, making it more than four times the cost of regular ramyun. That steep price tag put it out of reach for most consumers, and as a result, it struggled to gain popularity.

Samyang Cup Ramyun ad in 1970s

By the late 1970s, though, things were changing. As household incomes grew and electric hot water dispensers became more common, people began looking for quick, ready-to-eat meals. Sensing the shift, Nongshim jumped in. In 1981, they launched Sabalmyun, and a year later, rebranded it as *Yukgaejang Sabalmyun*—adding a gently spiced twist.

1981 Sabalmyun launch ad

But why did *Yukgaejang Sabalmyun* take off while Samyang's *Cup Ramyun* didn't? One major factor was the bowl shape. In Japan, it's common to lift your bowl while eating. But in Korea, traditional table manners say bowls should stay on the table.

Japanese drama Midnight Diner

Korean drama Let's Eat

Samyang's *Cup Ramyun* followed the Japanese design, which felt unfamiliar to many Korean consumers back then. *Sabalmyun*, on the other hand, was made to be eaten right from the table—just like a proper Korean meal.

Ansung Tang Myun 안성탕면

A Simple Classic with Deep Roots

After introducing Korea's first instant noodle, Samyang dominated the ramyun market for nearly two decades. Many competitors tried to break through—including Lotte Manufacturing, a company founded by a Korean-Japanese entrepreneur with operations in both Japan and Korea. In the late 1960s, Lotte launched its own instant noodles to challenge Samyang, but couldn't shake the powerhouse's reputation.

By the 1970s, Lotte made a strategic pivot. It rebranded its noodle division as *Nongshim*, meaning "farmer's sincere heart," in an effort to build a friendlier, more approachable image. At the time, nearly half of South Korea's economy was rooted in agriculture—making the new name especially fitting.

To take on the seemingly unbeatable Samyang, Nongshim doubled down on one thing: broth. They built a dedicated soup factory in Ansung, a city near Seoul known for its access to fresh ingredients from nearby farmland. The name *Ansung Tang Myun* comes from that city.

The strategy worked. In 1983, Nongshim launched *Ansung Tang Myun*, featuring a complex, miso-based broth that stood out from everything else on the market. It was an instant hit. By 1985, Nongshim had officially overtaken Samyang, claiming the No.1 spot in the *ramyun* industry—and holding onto it ever since.

Before *Shin Ramyun* stole the spotlight, Korea was living in the age of *Ansung Tang Myun*.

Interestingly, even after *Shin Ramyun* took over most of the country, *Ansung Tang Myun* held onto its throne in one region—Gyeongsang Province in the south.

South Korea

Gyeongsang Province

Why Gyeongsang Locals Strongly Prefer It

This regional loyalty puzzled many, but Nongshim offered a clear explanation. Gyeongsang cuisine has long featured rich, fermented flavors—especially *doenjang* (된장, soybean paste)—making *Ansung Tang Myun*'s savory broth a natural fit for the local palate.

Take *soondae* (Korean blood sausage), for example. In Gyeongsang Province, people dip it in soybean paste, while in the Seoul metropolitan

area, most use salt. It's a long-standing food debate—and Gyeongsang locals wouldn't dream of choosing salt.

How to Make Beef Miso Ramen with Ansung Tang Myun

Ansung Tang Myun's miso-based broth pairs beautifully with beef—especially grilled, thinly sliced brisket (*chadolbagi*, 차돌박이) and garlic. Here's how to take it up a notch:

1. Pan-fry thin slices of brisket and garlic until lightly crisp.
2. Cook the noodles according to the package instructions.
3. Top the bowl with the brisket, chopped green onions, and a dash of black pepper.
4. Serve hot and enjoy a heartier take on this comfort food!

Neoguri 너구리

The Noodle with a Quirky Name and a Bold Flavor

Released in 1982, *Neoguri* was Korea's first udon-style instant noodle—arriving a year before *Ansung Tang Myun*.

At the time, Nongshim was still the long-standing runner-up in the *ramyun* market and was ready to shake things up with something completely new.

Their plan was to introduce thick, chewy noodles paired with a light, seafood-based broth—a combination that didn't exist on the market yet.

Regular ramyun vs. Neoguri noodles

But bringing that concept to life wasn't easy. Doubling the thickness of regular *ramyun* noodles while keeping them chewy and quick-cooking posed a serious technical challenge. After countless trials, Nongshim finally perfected the formula—and *Neoguri* was born.

At launch, *Neoguri* was nearly twice the price of other *ramyun*—a bold move for the early '80s. But its unique texture and rich toppings quickly won people over, turning it into an unexpected hit.

1983 Neoguri ad emphasizing Udon-style noodles

The Kelp Factor

And then there was the kelp—an unexpected but unforgettable touch. Nongshim included a whole piece of *dasima* (다시마, kelp), sourced from Wando—an island that produces over 70% of Korea's kelp. It didn't just deepen the seafood flavor; it added a savory richness and made the broth more visually appealing.

For international versions, the kelp is finely chopped and blended into the soup base—a small adjustment made to suit local preferences.

Even today, many people still wonder whether the kelp is meant to be eaten or simply used to flavor the broth. A Nongshim survey found that 36% use it just for flavoring and toss it out, while the rest enjoy it as part of the meal. Nongshim proudly highlights its quality and encourages everyone to savor it.

So, Why the Name "Neoguri"?

The story behind *Neoguri*'s name begins with its concept. In 1982, the team at Nongshim was inspired by Japan's *Sanuki Udon*, known for its firm, al-dente texture. While brainstorming, they also looked at *Tanuki Udon*— a different dish with a fun-sounding name.

Sanuki Udon

Tanuki Udon

And that's how they landed on *Neoguri* (너구리), the Korean word for raccoon. The name was fun, quirky, and instantly memorable.

Back then—and even now—it stood out in a sea of more traditional names. That bold branding gave *Neoguri* a distinct identity, helping it become one of Korea's most recognizable and beloved instant noodles.

Chapagetti 짜파게티

Sweet, Savory, and Uniquely Korean-Chinese

Chapagetti is the instant noodle version of *jjajangmyeon*, one of Korea's most iconic comfort foods with roots in Korean-Chinese cuisine.

Jjajangmyeon originated with Chinese immigrants in Incheon. In the late 1800s, after Incheon opened its port to foreign trade, many Chinese immigrants settled in the area, bringing their culinary traditions with them.

One of the famous Chinese diners in Incheon (1955)

At first, they served traditional *zhájiàngmiàn* (炸酱面)—hand-pulled noodles tossed in black bean sauce. It was simple, adaptable, and easy to prepare with whatever ingredients were available.

Over time, the recipe evolved to suit Korean tastes, becoming the *jjajangmyeon* we know today—rich, savory, slightly sweet, and uniquely Korean. With its warm, comforting flavor, it quickly became a beloved everyday dish.

Jjajangmyeon 짜장면

In 1984, Nongshim brought that flavor to instant noodles with *Chapagetti*—a name that combines *"jjajangmyeon"* and *"spaghetti."*
It wasn't an exact replica of the original, but its powdered black bean sauce captured the essence in a milder, more approachable form. Its slightly sweet, savory flavor appealed to all ages—and it quickly caught on, even beyond Korea.

What Jjajangmyeon Means to Koreans

Up until the 1970s, *jjajangmyeon* was a go-to dish for celebrating graduations, birthdays, and other small milestones. While it was considered affordable, many families in post-war Korea still struggled financially, and *jjajangmyeon* offered a delicious yet budget-friendly way to mark a special day.

Buan Independent News

Mail News

Over time, the dish shifted from celebration food to an everyday staple—fast, satisfying, and deeply familiar. In Korean dramas and films, it often shows up during hectic workdays or emotionally charged scenes, adding a grounded, relatable touch.

Memories of Murder

Very Ordinary Couple

The Attorney

Lies Hidden in My Garden

One quirky tradition is eating *jjajangmyeon* on moving day. It's a common scene in K-dramas: characters sitting among unpacked boxes, sharing bowls of noodles in their new home.

TV show scenes depicting people eating jjajangmyeon on moving day

Why *jjajangmyeon*? Simple—when your tableware is still packed, delivery is the easiest choice. And in Korea, *jjajangmyeon* has long been a top pick for moments like these.

Given how deeply it's woven into everyday life, it's no surprise that *jjajangmyeon* was one of the first dishes recreated as an instant noodle. *Chapagetti* led the way in 1984, opening the door for newer, premium, and creative instant versions. But despite all the competition, *Chapagetti* still reigns as the undisputed king of instant *jjajangmyeon*.

A Little Chat About Chapagetti in the Movie Parasite

Chapagetti gained global attention after its appearance in the Oscar-winning film Parasite (2019). In one memorable scene, the wealthy housewife asks her helper to prepare *Jjapaguri*—also known as *Ramdon*—a mashup of two popular instant noodles: *Chapagetti* and *Neoguri*.

To elevate it, she asks the helper to add slices of Hanwoo, Korea's prized premium beef. The contrast is deliberate: *Chapagetti*, a symbol of everyday comfort, is paired with one of the country's most luxurious ingredients. The result is both clever and revealing—a subtle commentary on class and taste.

Movie Parasite

Jjapaguri (Ramdon)
차파구리

How to Make the Viral Jjapaguri (Serves 2)

1. Boil 500ml (17oz) of water and cook *Chapagetti* and Neoguri noodles for about 4 minutes. (Tip: If you use more water, you'll need to drain it before adding the seasonings.)
2. While the noodles cook, sauté diced beef to your liking.
3. When the noodles are nearly done, add 1 *Chapagetti* sauce packet, olive oil, and half the Neoguri soup base. Stir well.
4. Add the cooked beef and mix everything over low heat for 1 minute.
5. Serve hot and enjoy!

Bibim Men 비빔면

The Unrivaled King of Cold Noodles

The early 1980s marked the beginning of the instant noodle wars. Nongshim launched back-to-back mega-hit brands, eventually dethroning Samyang, which had dominated the market for decades.

As a newcomer, Paldo knew they had to take a different path to stand out among these giants. So they made a bold move—introducing something no one saw coming: an instant version of *bibim-guksu*, Korea's beloved cold noodle dish.

In Korean, *bibim* means "mixed," and *guksu* means "noodles." Much like *bibimbap*—which mixes rice with toppings and chili paste (*gochujang*, 고추장)— *bibim-guksu* is its noodle counterpart: refreshing, spicy, and packed with flavor.

Bibim-guksu 비빔국수

Originally, this dish was a royal delicacy called *Goldongmyeon* (골동면) during the Joseon Dynasty (*goldong* meaning "mixed"). Made with buckwheat noodles, beef, vegetables, soy sauce, and sesame oil, it was a luxury reserved for the upper class, since wheat was scarce at the time.

Goldongmyeon 골동면

After the Korean War, wheat flour became widely available, and *bibim-guksu* made its way into everyday homes. Over time, people began adding *gochujang* or kimchi for a spicy kick. Today, unless it's specifically described as soy-sauce-based, *bibim-guksu* almost always refers to the chili-based version.

Crafting the Perfect Bibim Sauce

Since *bibim-guksu* is a flexible dish that people often customize with whatever's in the fridge, Paldo knew that the sauce would make or break the instant version. To get it right, the team traveled across Korea, visiting restaurants famous for their cold noodles and testing flavor profiles until they nailed the perfect balance of spicy, tangy, and sweet.

The result was a bold innovation for its time: a liquid seasoning packet made using fermentation and microbial engineering techniques—something rarely seen in instant noodles back then.

When *Bibim Men* first hit store shelves, it made waves. But there was one small hiccup: many people didn't realize it was meant to be served cold, and mistakenly prepared it like regular hot, soupy ramyun.

To clear up the confusion, Paldo launched a TV ad campaign featuring a catchy jingle: *"Right-hand mixing, left-hand mixing, or mix with both hands!"*

The tune became an instant cultural hit—and stuck in consumers' heads for decades.

A 1984 TV commercial explaining how to properly eat Bibim Men

How to Enjoy Bibim Men

1. Boil the noodles for 3 minutes.
2. Rinse the cooked noodles under ice-cold water 2-3 times until fully chilled, then drain thoroughly (Too much leftover water can dilute the flavor!)
3. Mix the noodles with the liquid seasoning and top with a boiled egg, grilled meat, and your choice of fresh veggies.

Shin Ramyun 신라면

The King of Korean Instant Noodles

If you're reading this book, chances are you've seen, heard of, or even tried *Shin Ramyun*—now sold in over 120 countries and still growing strong.

By the early 1980s, Nongshim had already secured its place as the leading instant noodle brand in Korea, thanks to back-to-back hits like *Neoguri* (1982), *Ansung Tang Myun* (1983), and *Chapagetti* (1984). But to stay on top, it needed something new—something that had never been done before.

So Nongshim set out to create Korea's first truly spicy ramyun, inspired by the deep, rich flavors of *Sogogi Jangkuk* (소고기 장국), a traditional Korean beef stew. To emphasize the heat, they named it *Shin Ramyun* (辛 라면)—with the character 辛(Shin) meaning "spicy" —and wrapped it in striking red and black packaging to make its fiery kick unmistakable.

Sogogi Jangkuk 소고기 장국
A hearty beef stew made with brisket, Korean bean paste (Doenjang 된장), and red pepper paste (Gochujang 고추장)

To reinforce its bold image, Nongshim launched ad campaigns featuring the now-legendary tagline: *"Shin Ramyun, the ramen that makes tough men cry."*

1980s ad featuring the iconic tagline

2023 ad with soccer player Son Heung-Min using the same tagline

The slogan played off an old Korean saying: *"Men should cry only three times in their life"*—when they're born, when their parents pass away, and when their country falls.

Shin Ramyun playfully added a fourth reason: its intense heat. The message struck a chord, tapping into Koreans' pride in their love of spice. The branding worked—*Shin Ramyun* didn't just become a hit; it redefined what spicy ramyun meant in Korea.

Evolving with the Times

As times changed, so did cultural attitudes. The "tough men cry" slogan, once seen as clever, began to feel outdated to younger generations who were more conscious of gender stereotypes.

So in 2024, after 38 years, Nongshim officially retired the tagline and introduced a new theme: *"A ramen that fills life deliciously."*

The latest ads shifted the focus from toughness to togetherness—portraying *Shin Ramyun* as a versatile, everyday comfort for all kinds of moments, big or small. Instead of relying on celebrity endorsements, the commercials featured everyday people enjoying *Shin Ramyun* in their real lives—at home, at work, or on the go.

2024 Shin Ramyun TV Commercials Embracing the New Theme

Ambition for the Global Market

Shin Ramyun is no longer just Korea's favorite—it's becoming a global brand. In 2023, more than 60% of its total sales came from overseas markets, and that number keeps rising. And the U.S. is leading the way.

When Nongshim first brought *Shin Ramyun* to the U.S., there was internal debate: Should they tone down the heat to suit American tastes?

At the time, spicy instant noodles were rare in the U.S., and a milder version might have appealed to more people. But Nongshim stuck to the original recipe, betting on authenticity to set them apart. It was a bold move—and it worked!

What began in Korean grocery stores soon expanded to Asian supermarkets, then to mainstream retailers. Today, over 40% of *Shin Ramyun* buyers in the U.S. are non-Asian consumers—a clear sign that Korean spice has gone mainstream.

Shin Ramyun promo event
at Walmart, U.S.

Shin Ramyun stocked at
Costco, U.S.

Now one of America's top three instant noodle brands, *Shin Ramyun* is setting its sights on Europe. Will Europeans embrace spicy ramyun just as enthusiastically?

No one knows for sure—but as Nongshim pushes forward, many Koreans are cheering them on, hopeful that *Shin Ramyun* will become the No. 1 instant ramen brand in the world.

Shin Ramyun pop-up at
Carrefour, France

Nongshim set up European HQ in
Amsterdam, Netherlands

Viral Shin Ramyun Recipe

If you've never tried *Shin Ramyun* or are worried about the spice, there's a viral hack that gives it a creamy, cheesy twist: *Shin Ramyun Toowoomba.*

Toowoomba Pasta was originally created by the American chain Outback Steakhouse, named after an Australian region, and it became wildly popular in South Korea!

The recipe became such a hit online that Nongshim eventually released an official *Too(woo)mba* flavor—no cooking required! But if you can't find it, no worries—you can easily make your own using the original *Shin Ramyun.*

How to Make Shin Ramyun Toowoomba Pasta

1. Cook the *Shin Ramyun* noodles halfway, then drain and set aside.
2. In a pan, sauté chopped garlic and onion in olive oil until lightly browned. Add shrimp and cook until pink.
3. Pour in 250 ml (8 oz) of milk, a knob of butter, and a pinch of black pepper.
4. Stir in ½ to 1 packet of the soup base, depending on your spice preference.
5. Add two slices of cheddar cheese and stir until melted and creamy.
6. Add the noodles and mix for 1 minute until fully coated.
7. Garnish with parsley and enjoy!

Dosirac 도시락

A Nostalgic Korean Noodle Beloved in Russia

By the early 1980s, *Yukgaejang Sabalmyeon* had dominated Korea's cup noodle market, leaving little room for competitors. But in 1986, Paldo introduced a bold new challenger: *Dosirac*—which means "lunchbox" in Korean.

To stand out from *Yukgaejang Sabalmyeon, Dosirac* took a different route. Instead of the typical round cup, it came in a rectangular container—a first in Korea. Paldo also skipped the usual spicy kick in favor of a milder, savory broth, aiming to appeal to those craving something more subtle.

1980s Dosirac ad with the tagline:
"Both the look and flavor are unique!"

The new design and gentler flavor earned *Dosirac* a loyal fanbase—but it still couldn't unseat *Yukgaejang Sabalmyeon* at home.

Then came a surprising breakthrough—one that changed everything.

A Lucky Break in Russia

When Korea and Russia established diplomatic ties in the 1990s, Russian traders traveling by train discovered *Dosirac*. Its stackable rectangular shape made it easy to pack in bags—and convenient to eat on bumpy trains and boats.

Dosirac ad in Russia

The warm, mild broth was a perfect fit for Russia's cold climate, and it quickly won over local tastebuds.

As word spread, demand skyrocketed. In 1997, Paldo opened a small office in Vladivostok with just two employees managing operations.

By the end of that year, *Dosirac*'s sales had increased sevenfold—and continued growing at over 10% annually. Since 2013, *Dosirac* has sold more than 30 times as much in Russia as in South Korea.

The Secret to Market Domination

Today, *Dosirac* holds over 60% of Russia's cup noodle market—making it nearly impossible for competitors to catch up.

Its success comes down to smart, aggressive localization. Paldo adapted its offerings to Russian preferences, introducing milder flavors like beef, pork, chicken, and shrimp. But they didn't stop there—when they learned that many Russians enjoyed adding mayonnaise to their noodles, Paldo launched *Dosirac Plus*, complete with a mayo packet inside.

Thanks to these thoughtful adjustments, *Dosirac* has become synonymous with cup noodles in Russia—a rare achievement for any foreign brand.

Russian-Style Dosirac Recipe

1. Sprinkle the soup powder and dried vegetable packets over the *Dosirac* noodles.
2. Add sliced hot dog-style sausage.
3. Pour in hot water, cover, and let sit for 2 minutes.
4. Drizzle with mayonnaise, stir well, and enjoy!

Jin Ramen 진라면

The Second in Command, Challenging Shin Ramyun

When *Jin Ramen* launched in 1988, it barely made a ripple. Few believed it could ever stand a chance against the reigning champion, *Shin Ramyun*.

But today, *Jin Ramen* has emerged as *Shin Ramyun*'s biggest challenger. Between 2009 and 2018, it steadily gained ground—narrowing the gap and winning over fans.

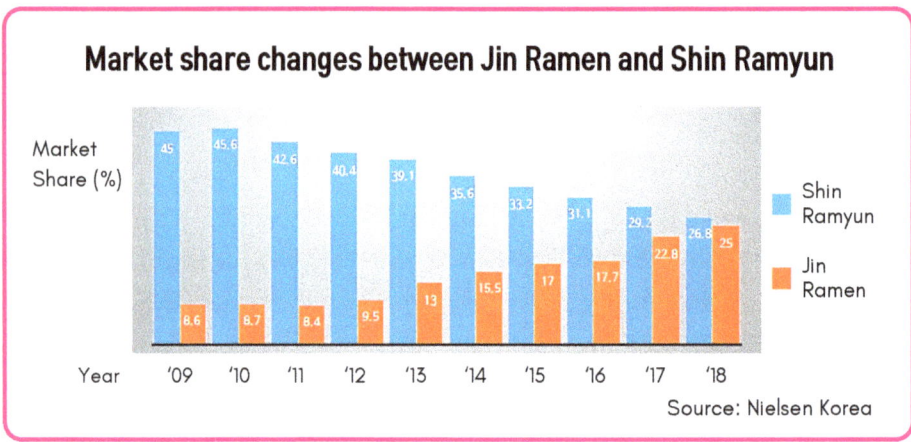

Market share changes between Jin Ramen and Shin Ramyun

Market Share (%)

Year	'09	'10	'11	'12	'13	'14	'15	'16	'17	'18
Shin Ramyun	45	45.6	42.6	40.4	39.1	35.6	33.2	31.1	29.2	26.8
Jin Ramen	8.6	8.7	8.4	9.5	13	15.5	17	17.7	22.8	25

Source: Nielsen Korea

The Secrets Behind Its Success

Jin Ramen was crafted with a rich, hearty broth designed to suit Korean tastes. Its name comes from the Korean verb *jinhada* (진하다), meaning "rich" or "deep," a nod to its bold, flavorful base.

Available in two versions—spicy and mild—it appeals to a wide range of eaters. With its deep broth and chewy noodles that stay firm after cooking, *Jin Ramen* has become a comfort food across generations.

Jin Ramen's mild and rich broth pairs perfectly with an egg

To strengthen its appeal among younger consumers, *Jin Ramen* teamed up with major celebrities like MLB pitcher Ryu Hyun-jin and K-pop superstar BTS's Jin, cleverly playing on the name while tapping into global fandoms.

K-pop idol BTS member Jin

MLB pitcher Ryu Hyun-Jin

But *Jin Ramen*'s rise isn't just about star power. Much of its success can be credited to Ottogi, the company behind it. The brand is widely respected in Korea for its ethical practices, consumer-friendly policies, and commitment to social responsibility—values that resonate deeply with Korean consumers and have helped *Jin Ramen* build a loyal following.

How to Make Jin Ramen Mazesoba

1. In a small sauce bowl, mix:
   - ½ packet of seasoning powder
   - 1 packet of dried veggies
   - A pinch of black pepper
   - 1 tbsp minced garlic & chili flakes

Korean Seaweed

2. Pan-fry 150g (about 5 oz) of minced pork with a bit of salt and pepper fully until cooked.
3. Stir 1 tbsp soy sauce into the seasoning mix (from step 1), then add the mixture to the pan. Turn off the heat and combine well.
4. Cook the noodles, drain, and toss with the sauce. Add 2-3 spoons of noodle water if needed.
5. Top with chopped scallions, garlic chives, crushed Korean seaweed snack (optional), and a raw egg yolk.
6. Mix well and enjoy!

Why Do Koreans Support Ottogi?

Of course, *Jin Ramen* has a long history and a flavor that's been perfected over time—winning over more and more fans. But Ottogi's rise isn't just about taste. Its reputation as *"Godtogi"* (갓뚜기)—a nickname blending "God" and "Ottogi"—has played a major role in its success.

Since its founding by the late Ham Tae-ho, Ottogi has consistently emphasized social responsibility. One standout moment came when ownership passed to his son, Ham Young-joon. Unlike many major conglomerates, Ottogi openly disclosed—and fully paid—a massive inheritance tax over the course of five years.

Ottogi's CEO Ham Young-joon

This rare act of transparency and accountability struck a chord with the public. Stories of Ottogi's business ethics went viral on social media, and more people began supporting the brand—not just for its noodles, but for what it stood for.

That groundswell of goodwill resonated deeply with Korean consumers. In 2017, Ottogi's market share jumped by 5%—a significant leap in Korea's fiercely competitive ramyun industry.

In Korea, moral integrity carries weight. Whether you're a singer, an athlete, or a CEO, skill alone isn't enough to earn long-term respect. Ethical conduct matters—and it has to be visible.

That belief applies to companies, too. Ottogi's consistent commitment to doing the right thing earned it both the nickname Godtogi and the loyalty of values-driven consumers. In doing so, Ottogi didn't just boost its own reputation—it raised the bar, encouraging other companies to take social responsibility more seriously.

Sari Gomtang 사리곰탕면 &
Gomtang 진국설렁탕면 Mild Comfort in a Bowl

By now, you might be wondering: Are all Korean instant noodles spicy? While many are, there are also a few mild, comforting options worth trying. Two popular choices are Nongshim's *Sari Gomtang* and Paldo's *Gomtang*.

Sari Gomtang
사리곰탕면

Gomtang
진국설렁탕면

Interestingly, Paldo's *Gomtang* is actually called *Jinguk Sullungtang Myun* (진국설렁탕면) in Korea. *Jinguk* means "authentic," *Sullungtang* refers to a traditional milky beef bone soup, and *Myun* means "noodles."

So why call it *Gomtang* in international markets instead of *Sullungtang*? Most likely, it comes down to ease of pronunciation and familiarity. *Gomtang* is simpler for non-Korean speakers to say and remember. Plus, by the time Paldo expanded overseas, Nongshim's *Sari Gomtang* had already gained recognition abroad—so sticking with the name *Gomtang* made sense.

Though *Sari Gomtang* has led Korea's white broth instant noodle market since 1988, Paldo's *Jinguk Sullungtang Myun* (internationally known as *Gomtang*) actually debuted earlier, in 1986. At the time, Nongshim chose *Gomtang* for its product name because Paldo had already claimed *Sullungtang*.

Gomtang vs. Sullungtang: What's the Difference?

Gomtang is a traditional Korean soup made by simmering beef cuts like brisket and shank for 3-4 hours, resulting in a clear, light broth. *Sullungtang*, on the other hand, is made by boiling ox bones for over 12 hours, producing a rich, milky-white soup.

Historically, *Gomtang* was considered a luxury dish, as beef cuts were expensive, while *Sullungtang* was more of an everyday meal—made from affordable ox bones and often shared among large families. Since both instant noodle versions are based on beef bone broth, their flavor leans more toward *Sullungtang* than *Gomtang*.

Gomtang 곰탕

Sullungtang 설렁탕

They're delicious on their own—but for an upgrade, try turning them into *Tteok Mandu Guk* (Rice Cake and Dumpling Soup, 떡만두국).

How to Make Tteok Mandu Guk (Rice Cake & Dumpling Soup)

1. Boil water, then add sliced rice cakes and frozen dumplings (adjust timing based on dumpling size).
2. When it boils again, add *Sari Gomtang* or *Gomtang* noodles.
3. Once cooked, garnish with green onion, egg strips, and black pepper.

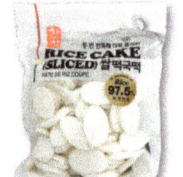

Sliced Rice Cakes

Steamed/Soup Dumplings

- **Sliced Rice Cake**
These thinly sliced rice cakes (*tteok*) are perfect for soups and stews. Add them to kimchi stew or *army stew* for extra chew and heartiness.

- **Soup Dumplings**
Bibigo has quickly become the top name in Korea's dumpling game—worth a try if you're curious!

The Meaning Behind Tteok Guk & Tteok Mandu Guk

Tteok Guk 떡국

In Korea, families celebrate Lunar New Year by holding ancestral rites and eating *tteokguk* (rice cake soup, 떡국). These days, many households add dumplings, turning it into *tteok mandu guk* (rice cake and dumpling soup, 떡만두국)—but traditionally, *tteokguk* is served on its own.

There's a popular saying: *"You become a year older after eating tteokguk."*

Kids love this idea and eagerly finish their bowls, hoping to grow taller—or feel just a little more grown-up.

This New Year's tradition is rich with symbolism. The pure white broth represents brightness and fresh beginnings—an invitation to leave the old year behind and start anew.

Kyunghyang News

Children in traditional Korean hanbok enjoying Tteok Guk

Garae Tteok 가래떡

Even the ingredients carry meaning — long, white garae tteok (가래떡), cylinder-shaped rice cakes, represent longevity, while the thin, coin-like slices symbolize wealth.

Together, *tteokguk* reflects hopes for a long life and prosperity in the year ahead.

Anchovy Kal Guk Soo 멸치 칼국수

A Healthier, Non-Spicy Classic

When it hit shelves in 1997, *Anchovy Kal Guk Soo* stood out by offering something refreshingly different: a mild, non-spicy take on Korea's traditional *kal guk soo*, made with air-dried noodles instead of the usual fried ones.

Seafood Kal Guk Soo
해물 칼국수

At a time when most Korean *ramyun* focused on bold, spicy flavors, Nongshim set its sights on something lighter—mild, lower in calories, and built around a clean broth. The simple, health-conscious look caught shoppers' eyes right away, and many were eager to try this new kind of noodle—especially those who had grown tired of fiery red broth.

As wellness trends exploded in the 2000s, air-dried noodles surged in popularity. Competitors released their own *kal guk soo*-inspired products, but none could top Nongshim's original. To this day, it remains the only *kal guk soo-style* instant noodle with lasting success in the market.

From Aristocratic Luxury to Everyday Comfort

Kal Guk Soo literally translates to "knife-cut noodles" (*kal* meaning knife, and *guk soo* meaning noodles), referring to the traditional method of hand-rolling and slicing dough with a knife.

Originally, *kal guk soo* was a luxury food enjoyed by Korea's upper class, as wheat flour was scarce and expensive.

Love.seoul.go.kr

Things changed after the Korean War. As part of its aid program, the U.S. supplied large amounts of wheat flour, making it widely available across Korea. *Kal guk soo* soon became a popular market dish—affordable, filling, and comforting.

Kal Guk Soo Alley in a Traditional Korean Market

Today, *kal guk soo* comes in countless regional variations. Specialty restaurants serve everything from rich, bone-based broths to seafood versions made with clams and anchovies. Among these, the anchovy and seafood broth style remains one of the most beloved in modern Korean cuisine.

Anchovy Kal Guk Soo is great on its own, but with a few easy upgrades, you can turn it into a restaurant-style bowl of *clam kal guk soo* (바지락 칼국수).

How to Make Clam Kal Guk Soo

1. Rinse the clams by scrubbing them with salt, then soak them in saltwater in a dark place to purge any sand.
2. Wash and julienne the carrots and zucchini.
3. In a pot, bring the recommended amount of water (per the package instructions) to a boil with the pre-soaked clams.
4. Once boiling, add the noodles, seasoning packets, zucchini, carrots, and minced garlic (optional). Simmer for 5 minutes.
5. Serve hot with fresh Kimchi for the perfect balance of flavors!

Rabokki 라볶이

The Ultimate Korean Soul Food

Rabokki might not be one of the top-selling instant noodles, but we have to talk about it—along with its older sibling, *Tteokbokki* (떡볶이)—because it's one of Korea's ultimate soul foods.

Let's break it down: *tteok* means rice cake, and *bokki* means stir-fried dish. Traditional tteokbokki features chewy rice cakes, fish cakes, and green onions stir-fried in a sweet and spicy *gochujang* (고추장) sauce.

Rabokki, on the other hand, throws *ramyun* noodles into the mix—or, for many, it's the perfect combo of rice cakes *and* noodles in one glorious bowl.

Think of *rabokki* as the noodle-powered version of one of Korea's longtime street food staples. Paldo introduced the first instant *rabokki* in 2012, and today, many brands offer their own take on this cult classic.

For non-Koreans, *tteokbokki* and *rabokki* can be a love-it-or-hate-it experience. Some aren't into the chewy texture of the rice cakes, the sweetness of the sauce, or the sheer carb overload.

But to be honest—it's not exactly healthy food. It's pure comfort: carbs drenched in sweet, spicy sauce. And that's exactly what makes it so irresistible to Koreans.

A Brief History of Tteokbokki

Tteokbokki has royal roots—it began as a soy sauce-based dish with braised beef and rice cakes, served in the royal court.

Traditional Royal Court Tteokbokki

After the Korean War, street vendors in Sindang-dong gave it a bold twist, swapping the soy sauce for spicy *gochujang*. This new version quickly gained popularity and spread across the country. Today, Sindang-dong is still known for its *tteokbokki* snack bars that line the streets.

Sindang-dong Tteokbokki Town

Over time, *tteokbokki* has taken on all kinds of creative flavors—there's carbonara *tteokbokki*, curry *tteokbokki*, *jjajang* (black bean sauce) *tteokbokki*, and even rosé or cream-based versions. Still, for most Koreans, the classic *gochujang*-based style remains the ultimate go-to.

Sindang-dong Style Tteokbokki, cooked directly at your own table

How to Upgrade Rabokki

Rice Cakes   *Fish Cakes*

1. Prepare a boiled egg for topping—it pairs perfectly with the sweet and spicy sauce.
2. In a pot, boil water and cook the noodles, rice cakes, and fish cakes (optional) for about 3–4 minutes.
3. When the noodles and rice cakes are nearly done, drain most of the water, leaving about 3–4 spoonfuls in the pot.
4. Add the sauce packet, toss in thinly sliced green onions, and turn off the heat.
5. Stir everything together until well coated. Enjoy hot!

Buldak 불닭볶음면

Infamously Spicy and Impossible to Resist

It's finally time to talk about the legendary *Buldak*! Released in 2012, it's a relatively recent addition to the instant noodle world—but it quickly became a global phenomenon.

Its full Korean name, 불닭볶음면 (*Buldak Bokkeum-myun*), translates to "fire chicken stir-fried noodles." *Bul* means fire, *dak* means chicken, and *bokkeum-myun* refers to stir-fried noodles.

True to its name, *Buldak* delivers an intense, addictive heat that's won over spice lovers worldwide. You've probably seen the challenge videos—people sweating, crying, or gasping after just one bite.

Korean Englishman YouTube Channel

A Coreana Soyeon YouTube Channel

Hi Chad YouTube Channel

Most people say the first bite is surprisingly manageable—a sweet and savory flavor that masks the heat. But don't be fooled. The spice builds fast, becoming overwhelming for the unprepared.

In fact, *Buldak* was so intense that Denmark issued a recall and banned its sale in 2024. Ironically, the ban only fueled curiosity, sparking even more people to try it—and making *Buldak* even more famous.

Denmark recalls Korean ramen for being too spicy

Frances Mao
BBC News

12 June 2024

Denmark has recalled several spicy ramen noodle products by South Korean company Samyang, claiming that the capsaicin levels in them could poison consumers.

Source: BBC News

The Visionary Behind Buldak

The mastermind behind this global sensation is Kim Jung-soo, vice chairwoman of Samyang Foods and daughter-in-law of the company's founder, the late Jeon Joong-yoon.

In 1998, during Korea's financial crisis, Kim joined Samyang to support her husband, Jeon In-jang, after the company faced bankruptcy.

The idea for *Buldak* struck her in 2010 while taking a walk with her daughter. She noticed a long line outside a stir-fried rice restaurant famous for its extreme spiciness. Intrigued, she tried the dish herself and immediately saw its potential.

The fiery heat was unlike anything she'd tasted before, and she became determined to recreate that flavor in instant noodle form.

She didn't waste time. Kim headed straight to the supermarket, bought three of every spicy sauce and seasoning she could find, and sent them to Samyang's research and marketing teams.

From there, the food development team went all in—testing 1,200 chickens, two tons of sauce, and chili peppers from around the world to perfect the recipe. They even visited Korea's spiciest restaurants to capture the essence of local heat.

After its launch in 2012, *Buldak* quickly gained traction through YouTube mukbang videos—live or recorded eating shows where hosts share their reactions to food—and endorsements from international K-pop stars like BTS and Blackpink. The buzz sent its popularity skyrocketing.

Before *Buldak*, Samyang Foods had struggled to compete with Korea's larger food giants, despite being the creator of the country's first instant noodle. But thanks to *Buldak*'s explosive global success, the company made a dramatic comeback and reclaimed its place in the spotlight.

BTS's Jimin eating Buldak cup noodles on Instagram

Blackpink's Rosé sharing her love for Buldak on Vogue France

How to Enjoy Buldak for Beginners

With *Buldak* becoming a global hit, Samyang has expanded the lineup with bold, fusion-inspired flavors to reach a broader audience. From curry and tomato pasta to habanero, tom yum, and cheese—these twists take instant noodles far beyond traditional Korean *ramyun*.

Curious but a little cautious? Start with *Buldak Carbonara* or *Buldak Cream Carbonara*. These milder versions offer a creamy, cheesy flavor that's perfect for first-timers. Even American singer Cardi B gave the Carbonara flavor a try and shared her reaction on social media—naturally, it went viral in Korea!

Feeling brave? Go for the original *Buldak*! To help balance the heat, add a fried egg and a slice of cheese—a popular combo known as *Bulgyechi* (불계치), short for *Buldak*, gyeran (egg), and cheese.

Even if you're a spice lover, save the 2x and 3x spicy versions for later. Start with the original, then work your way up!

Bulgyechi 불계치

A Fun Korean Idiom About Ramyun

Have you ever heard the phrase *"Do you want to eat ramyun (at my place)?"* (라면 먹을래요?) in a Korean drama or movie? On the surface, it sounds like a casual invite to share a late-night bite. But in certain contexts—especially between two people testing the waters of romance—it means a little more.

This phrase became famous after appearing in the Korean movie *One Fine Spring Day* (2001). In the film, the female lead thanks the male lead for driving her home and heads inside. But then, she suddenly returns to his car and asks, *"Do you want to eat ramyun?"* (implying at her place).

Movie One Fine Spring Day

Of course, they didn't just eat ramyun and call it a night! 😉

After the film's release, *"Do you want to eat ramyun?"* took on a new life as a playful, slightly provocative way to suggest taking things to the next level.

So if you're ever tempted to use the phrase with a Korean romantic interest—just make sure you know exactly what you're implying!

Snacks

Crunchy, Chewy, and Totally Addictive

Shrimp Crackers 새우깡

The All-Time Steadyseller

If *Shin Ramyun* is the undisputed king of Korean instant noodles, then *Shrimp Crackers* (*Saewookkang*, 새우깡) proudly wears the crown in the world of Korean snacks.

Launched in 1971, *Shrimp Crackers* became Korea's first bagged snack—at a time when the idea of pre-packaged snacks was still unfamiliar. Before that, Korean snack options were mostly limited to biscuits, hard candy, and *geonbbang* (건빵), a type of dry, army-style hardtack. So the arrival of *Shrimp Crackers* was a total game-changer.

The snack was originally developed by Lotte, before the company's noodle and snack division rebranded as Nongshim. Because Lotte operated in both Japan and Korea, many early Korean snack products were inspired by proven hits from Japan. *Shrimp Crackers* was no exception—it took inspiration from Calbee's popular *Kappa Ebisen*.

Japan's Kappa Ebisen (left) vs. Korea's Shrimp Crackers (right) - their evolution from launch to today

It took over a year for Lotte to develop the baking method used for *Shrimp Crackers*, which involved roasting them on heated salt instead of deep-frying. This gave the snack its signature light, savory flavor without the heaviness of oil—instantly setting it apart in the Korean market.

1970s Shrimp Cracker Ads

Its success was so massive, it even influenced Korea's shrimp industry. When the company switched from using Chinese-imported shrimp to sourcing from Korea, domestic shrimp demand soared. Later, when they shifted again to U.S. shrimp, the Korean shrimp market took a noticeable hit—showing just how powerful this snack had become.

Today, the snack aisle is overflowing with options, but *Shrimp Crackers* remains a steady favorite—especially among older generations who associate it with childhood nostalgia. Even now, it continues to rank as one of Korea's best-selling snacks, a testament to its lasting appeal.

Insider's Note

TV Drama Chocolate

In Korean dramas and movies, you'll often see characters pairing *Shrimp Crackers* with soju, Korea's iconic rice wine. It's a humble but meaningful combo that signals comfort and vulnerability.

When *Shrimp Crackers* and soju hit the screen, you know the characters are about to drop their walls and reveal their true feelings.

Kkul Kwabegi 꿀꽈배기

The Quiet Pioneer in Sweet Snacks

After making a big splash in the Korean snack market with savory *Shrimp Crackers* in 1971, Nongshim took a bold turn the following year— launching *Kkul Kwabegi*, a snack packed with sweet flavors.

The name comes from *kwabegi* (꽈배기), twisted Korean-style doughnuts. Originally, the snack was simply called *Kwabegi*, but in 1979, Nongshim added *kkul* (꿀), meaning "honey," to highlight its sweetness. In English-speaking countries, it's sold as *Honey Twist Snack*.

Kwabegi 꽈배기

At the time, most Korean snacks were either plain or salty, so a sweet, crunchy treat was still a novelty. But instead of overwhelming it with sugar, Nongshim kept the sweetness light and natural—using Korean acacia honey to create a flavor that wouldn't feel too heavy on the palate.

This subtle sweetness won over a wide range of consumers, helping *Kkul Kwabegi* quietly thrive for decades—without the help of flashy celebrity endorsements or major ad campaigns.

Now, instead of traditional advertising, Nongshim is leaning into playful, creative marketing. In 2024, they launched *Kkul Kwabegi Makgeolli*, a Korean rice wine inspired by the snack's flavor. It's a clever way to make traditional drinks more approachable for younger generations—while keeping the brand fresh with unexpected twists.

Choco Pie 초코파이

Korea's Symbol of "Jeong"

Choco Pie has been a beloved Korean snack ever since Orion introduced it in 1974. With its soft biscuit layers, marshmallow center, and chocolate coating, it's something almost every Korean has tried at least once—often tied to childhood memories, school field trips, or late-night cravings.

What makes *Choco Pie* truly unique, though, is how Orion skillfully linked the snack to the Korean concept of *Jeong* (정) through its branding.

If you look at the Korean packaging, you'll notice the Chinese character for *Jeong* (情). While the word has no perfect English translation, it describes a deep emotional bond—one rooted in affection, loyalty, and a quiet sense of belonging. *Jeong* is what connects people in Korea, often in subtle, unspoken ways.

Orion saw an opportunity to tap into this cultural core and marketed *Choco Pie* as "the snack that shares *Jeong*," paired with the famous slogan: *"I understand you without words"* (말하지 않아도 알아요).

It was more than clever marketing—it struck a chord. Over time, *Choco Pie* came to represent not just a sweet treat, but a gesture of care and connection. A symbol of something warm and quietly meaningful.

A Choco Pie ad featuring the theme of Jeong

A Ministry of Defense blog showing Choco Pie

A scene from the iconic film Joint Security Area, where a North Korean soldier takes a bite and says, "My wish is for North Korea to one day make snacks tastier than South Korea's. Until then, I'll have to keep longing for Choco Pie.

The Trademark Battle

Orion's *Choco Pie* didn't go unchallenged for long. By the late 1970s, Lotte released its own version, followed by Haitai in 1986 and Crown in 1989. All of them used the name *"Choco Pie,"* kicking off a fierce wave of competition.

| Orion | Lotte | Crown | No Brand |

Orion fought back and took the matter to court—but lost. The trademark they had registered only covered *"Orion Choco Pie,"* not *"Choco Pie"* as a standalone term. That left the door wide open. As long as competitors included their brand name, they could legally sell their own version of *Choco Pie*.

Realizing they couldn't win the battle over the name alone, rival companies began creating their own takes on chocolate-cream snacks to avoid going head-to-head with Orion (we'll dive into those on later pages!). Today, several brands still sell their own *Choco Pies*—but when people think of the name, Orion is still the one that comes to mind.

Choco Pie's Unexpected Role

Maybe it's because *Choco Pie* is so closely tied to *Jeong* (정), but in Korea, it's even used as a birthday cake! Whether it's for budget reasons, nostalgia, or just for fun, people love stacking up *Choco Pies*, sticking in a few candles, and surprising someone they care about.

Since *Choco Pies* are easy to find at any convenience store—and don't require cutting or plates—they've become the perfect last-minute party fix. You'll often see this in real life: in military barracks, dorm rooms, and classrooms—anywhere friends can gather, sing together, and celebrate with whatever candles they can find.

Movie Pawn

오늘도 누군가가
다시 미소 짓고

Choco Pie TV ad

TV drama Brewing Love

Choco Pie TV ad

But in the end, it's not really about the cake—it's about the gesture. A few Choco Pies, some good friends, and a little thoughtfulness are all it takes to make someone feel special.

Ace 에이스

Korea's First Cracker and a Timeless Favorite

Launched by Haitai Confectionery in 1974, Ace holds the title of Korea's very first cracker. With its rich, buttery flavor and light, crispy texture, Ace has remained a top-seller for decades—earning its place as a beloved classic.

In the 1970s, Korea's economy was booming, and eating habits were shifting with it. People were craving something new and more sophisticated, so Haitai decided to introduce a Western-style snack. In 1971, they launched *Johnny Cracker* (죠니 크랙카), inspired by American crackers.

But there was one problem—Koreans weren't used to the dry, hard texture of American-style crackers, so *Johnny Cracker* flopped hard. Rather than trying to salvage it, Haitai made a bold move: they scrapped it entirely and started fresh, determined to create a cracker Koreans would actually love.

They assembled a research team of eight experts, and after three years of trial and error, they struck gold—a cracker that was light, crisp, and flavorful without being overly dry. The team was so proud of the result that they named it Ace, meaning "the best" or "number one."

*Johnny Cracker
Magazine ad*

Early Ace crackers

Ace was an instant hit. Demand skyrocketed, and production lines ran 24/7—even on weekends—yet they still couldn't keep up. What's even crazier is that Ace was more than twice the price of instant noodles at the time, but people happily paid extra just to get their hands on it.

Then came a perfect pairing. In 1976, Maxwell House introduced instant coffee to Korea—and suddenly, Ace had a match. Coffee and Ace became a popular combo, especially in *dabang* (다방, traditional Korean coffee-houses), where trendy young people would sip coffee and snack on Ace.

Korea's coffeehouse scene in the 1970s

As Ace's popularity climbed, Haitai scored big in 1985 by featuring rising star Kim Hye-soo in its first TV commercial, cementing the cracker's status as a household name.

Kim Hye-soo, main model for Ace in the 1980s

To keep up with changing tastes, Haitai has rolled out new flavors over the years. They launched Ace Light (with 25% less fat), Ace Maecom (spicy), cheese, and vegetable flavors. None of these really gained traction—but Ace kept on going.

More recently, they've introduced more modern, dessert-style flavors like New York cheesecake, espresso con panna, and a lemony strawberry sand cake. Still, the original buttery classic remains the top pick for most consumers.

Will Ace ever create a new flavor that outruns the original and rewards all that effort? Who knows. What matters is that Ace keeps evolving—adapting to new lifestyles and preferences—so it can stay the perfect coffee companion for the next generation too.

Ojingeo Ddangkong 오징어 땅콩

The Ultimate Beer Snack and Beyond

For many outside Korea, the name *Ojingeo Ddangkong* probably sounds a little strange—it literally translates to "squid peanuts." *Ojingeo* (오징어) means squid, and *ddangkong* (땅콩) means peanut. For convenience, Koreans often just call it "*Ottang*" (오땅).

If you're from a culture that doesn't snack on dried squid, you might be thinking, "What kind of combo is this?" (Totally fair!) But in Korea, dried squid and peanuts are a familiar pairing—especially with beer. You'll find them on the menu at almost any pub.

insaengdomae.com

Naturally, *Ojingeo Ddangkong* quickly found its place as a favorite beer snack.

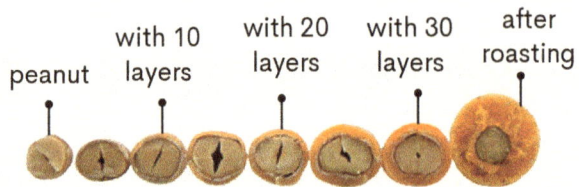

peanut — with 10 layers — with 20 layers — with 30 layers — after roasting

The process of making Ojingeo Ddangkong—
peanuts coated layer by layer with flour and syrup

Riding the success of Shrimp Crackers, Orion went with a simple, no-frills name based on the snack's two main ingredients to stand out on store shelves.

To boost its appeal, they cast rising teen star Lee Deok-hwa in early commercials. The catchy ads worked, and Ojingeo Ddangkong quickly became a hit.

Lee Deok-hwa in 1970s

Free bar snack of a copycat version

By the 2000s, copycat versions flooded the market. Many bars began serving cheaper imitations as free snacks alongside drinks.

To stay ahead, Orion launched a brand refresh. They introduced the slogan *"Sim-sim Free"*—a playful twist on *sim-sim-puli* (심심풀이, or "killing boredom")—to reposition *Ojingeo Ddangkong* as a fun, anytime snack, not just a beer companion. The new branding gave it a casual, everyday vibe that clicked with younger audiences.

2004 Ojingeo Ddangkong ad introducing its fresh new concept

At the same time, Orion leaned into the snack's legacy to distinguish it from imitators. In 2006, they added "Since 1976" to the packaging and promoted *Ojingeo Ddangkong* as the one and only original.

Today, whether you're sipping beer, watching a soccer match, or just craving something crunchy, *Ojingeo Ddangkong* remains a loyal companion—proof that some things never lose their charm.

Home Run Balls 홈런볼

The Taste of Childhood

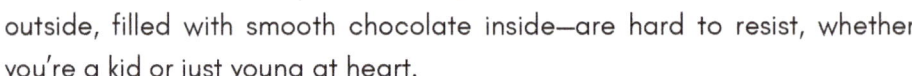

Home Run Balls have been a nostalgic favorite in Korea ever since Haitai introduced them in 1981. These bite-sized pastries—flaky on the outside, filled with smooth chocolate inside—are hard to resist, whether you're a kid or just young at heart.

As the name suggests, *Home Run Balls* were inspired by baseball. The original marketing featured mischievous cartoon characters and a playful, sporty theme, which made the snack instantly appealing.

Early 1990s Home Run Balls ad featuring its baseball theme

The timing couldn't have been better. Around the same time, Haitai's own baseball team, the Haitai Tigers, became a national powerhouse, dominating the league season after season. Their success added to the snack's sporty image and boosted its popularity even more.

Haitai Tigers, the dominant team from the 1980s to mid-1990s

With just the right balance of sweetness and clever marketing, *Home Run Balls* became a hit—not only with kids and teens, but also with adults drawn to their nostalgic charm. Over the years, Haitai experimented with fun flavors like tiramisu, cheese, caramel, melon, and strawberry. Most didn't last long, though—the original chocolate version remains the longtime favorite.

Home Run Balls in various flavors, though most were short-lived

What makes *Home Run Balls* especially appealing is their melt-in-your-mouth texture. The light, crispy layers and soft chocolate center create the perfect bite-sized indulgence. Since they're quiet to eat, students often sneak them into libraries or study rooms—so much so that it even inspired a fun commercial set in a library!

Library-themed Home Run Balls ad

And while they're great straight out of the bag, there's a new twist that's taken off on social media: toasting them in an air fryer. Just pop them in at 140°C (280°F) for 5 minutes, or 180°C (350°F) for 3 minutes. You'll get warm, toasty Home Run Balls with an even richer, more intense chocolate flavor. Definitely worth a try!

Pepero 빼빼로

The Snack That Became a Cultural Phenomenon

Just like *Shrimp Crackers*, *Pepero* was born during a time when Japanese snacks weren't officially available in Korea. In 1983, Lotte introduced Pepero, inspired by Japan's popular *Pocky* by Glico.

Pepero hit the market just as Koreans were craving new kinds of sweets and snacks. Its slim, chocolate-coated sticks in bright red packaging immediately stood out. At first, Lotte marketed it to kids, featuring cartoon characters and comedians in their ads. But as trends evolved, they shifted gears—enlisting top idol groups as brand ambassadors and aggressively expanding their market.

1980s Pepero TV commercials

Pepero's Clever Marketing Move

Of all of Lotte's marketing strategies, the creation of *Pepero Day* stands out as the most powerful—a brilliant move that turned November 11 into a nationwide celebration, where people gift *Pepero* to family, friends, and loved ones.

So, how did it begin? In 1994, students at a high school in Busan started exchanging *Pepero* sticks, joking that eating the slim snack might help them achieve "*Pepero-thin*" bodies. (Teenagers and their wild ideas, right?)

What started as a playful inside joke quickly spread, and on November 11 that year, *Pepero* sales in the region spiked. A local Lotte manager took note and passed it up to headquarters—sparking the next big idea. By the following year, Lotte launched a full-scale campaign, officially establishing November 11 as *Pepero Day*.

The promotion encouraged people to gift *Pepero* as a token of affection, and by 1996, media coverage had transformed it into a nationwide tradition. By the 2000s, *Pepero Day* had become such a phenomenon that it accounted for more than half of the snack's annual sales.

The impact was so strong that even Japan's Glico took notice. In 1999, they launched *Pocky Day* —clearly inspired by Korea's success. But while *Pepero Day* grew into a cultural tradition, *Pocky Day* remains mostly a marketing push in Japan.

Pepero Day promotion in Korea

Ambition to Go Global

As K-dramas, K-pop, and Korean food gained international popularity in the mid-2000s, *Pepero* rode the wave. Lotte didn't stay passive—they actively fueled the momentum, teaming up with K-pop idols and rolling out campaigns around the world.

Pepero Day ads featuring K-Pop idols New Jeans in New York's Times Square

Kko Kal Con 꼬깔콘

From American Roots to Korean Icon

Kko Kal Con might seem like just another cone-shaped corn snack today, but back in the early '80s, it was a bold and ambitious project for Lotte Confectionery.

In 1982, Lotte partnered with General Mills—the American company behind *Bugles*—to bring the snack to Korea. They built a large-scale production plant and even imported state-of-the-art machinery from the U.S. to manufacture *Kko Kal Con* locally.

The snack was a hit right out of the gate. By 1984, just a year after its debut, sales had doubled, and *Kko Kal Con* quickly became one of Lotte's top-selling products. One key reason for its early success was the unforgettable

TV commercials featuring Cho Yong-pil, Korea's biggest pop star at the time.

In the ads, he sang a catchy jingle while showing viewers the "right way" to eat *Kko Kal Con*—by sliding the cones onto his fingers and eating them one by one. This fun, finger-eating style caught on fast and remains a signature way to enjoy the snack even today.

Fast forward to today, and *Kko Kal Con* is still going strong. Its sales have grown more than 30 times since launch, securing its spot as the top corn snack in Korea's competitive market.

Kko Kal Con featured in the Korean drama, Reply 1988

The 1980s: When Western Culture Poured In

The 1980s in Korea were a time of major cultural shifts—a whirlwind of change, chaos, and excitement.

In 1980, following a military coup that ended 18 years of authoritarian rule, a new government came to power. To ease public discontent, it dramatically loosened restrictions on international travel and foreign cultural imports. Just months earlier, Western products had been banned in the name of patriotism. But almost overnight, the doors opened wide, and foreign music, movies, and consumer goods surged into Korean daily life.

This sudden influx of Western culture had a huge impact on food and snacks. Koreans were eager to try the treats they had only seen in movies or magazines. Companies responded quickly—launching new products inspired by global brands and featuring international celebrities in their ads.

At first, Hong Kong movie stars—wildly popular across Asia at the time—took center stage. One of the most talked-about examples was Chow Yun-fat's commercial for Milkis, which became a smash hit and helped usher more Hong Kong celebrities into Korean advertising.

Then in 1989, French actress Sophie Marceau became the first Western celebrity to appear in a Korean commercial.

Her appearance marked the beginning of a new era, with Western stars becoming a regular presence in Korean ads throughout the 1990s and beyond.

Oh Yes 오예스
& Mon Cher 몽쉘

Choco Pie's Biggest Rivals

Remember the Choco Pie we talked about earlier? Back then, Orion's trademark slip-up meant that other companies could also use the name "*Choco Pie*." Rivals like Haitai and Lotte jumped in, releasing their own versions of this national treat.

But Haitai took a different approach. Instead of going head-to-head, they chose to stand out. In 1984, they introduced *Oh Yes*, a new cream-filled chocolate cake. Unlike *Choco Pie*, which used marshmallows, *Oh Yes* featured a rich chocolate cream center and a sleek square shape—perfect for chocolate lovers who wanted something a little more indulgent. It quickly won over fans looking for something new.

Not to be outdone, Lotte aimed for the premium tier with *Mon Cher Tonton*. The French-inspired name (meaning "My Dear Uncle") was meant to add an upscale feel—but since "Tonton" sounded a bit like "chubby" in Korean, they eventually dropped it and stuck with *Mon Cher*. (In North America, you'll find it as *Moncher Dream Cake*.) Instead of marshmallow or chocolate cream, *Mon Cher* has a generous layer of smooth white cream, giving it a lighter, more velvety texture.

Oh Yes   Choco Pie   Mon Cher

Each treat has its own charm:

- **Oh Yes**: Light chocolate coating and cream with a soft, moist cake texture
- **Choco Pie**: Thick chocolate shell with a chewy marshmallow filling
- **Mon Cher**: Whipped white cream with a rich, smooth, cake-like feel

Since *Mon Cher* debuted in 1991, the rankings held steady for years—*Choco Pie* stayed at the top, *Mon Cher* in second, and *Oh Yes* in third. But in the 2020s, *Oh Yes* shook things up by launching unique flavors and bold new branding that clicked with younger consumers—climbing its way to second place.

Various unique flavors of Oh Yes

Of course, *Choco Pie* and *Mon Cher* didn't just sit back. Both brands have stayed relevant with limited editions and creative collaborations. With all three rolling out new flavors and standout campaigns, the snack rivalry is still going strong.

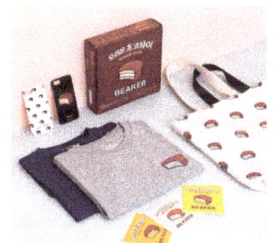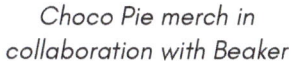

Choco Pie merch in collaboration with Beaker

Choco Pie House pop-up store at Hyundai Department Store

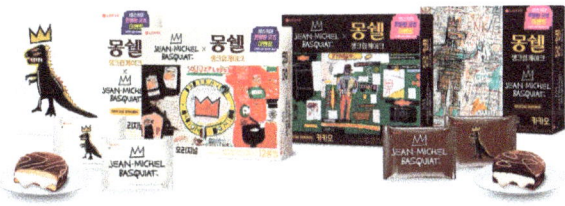

Mon Cher x Taegeukdang Bakery collaboration

Mon Cher x Jean-Michel Basquiat collaboration

Couque D'asse 쿠크다스

The Delicate Biscuit with an Unbreakable Fanbase

Couque D'asse, launched by Crown Confectionery in 1986, is one of Korea's most well-known biscuits.
Like many snacks from the '70s and '80s, it was inspired by a Japanese treat—Sanritsu's *Couque D'asse* (クックダッセ).

Sanritsu's
Couque D'asse

The name "*Couque D'asse*" roughly translates to "cookie from Asse," a town in Belgium. According to legend, when Belgium's King Leopold I entered Brussels, he tossed biscuits to the people as a gesture of goodwill. Whether or not that's the real origin of the name, it's Crown Confectionery's official story!

Of course, *Couque D'asse* isn't exactly a Belgian cookie—but the name helped frame it as a European-style luxury treat. Crown leaned into that image, with '80s ads designed to evoke the elegance and charm of Europe—or at least, how many Koreans imagined it at the time.

From the start, *Couque D'asse* stood out. Its light, buttery layers and creamy filling set it apart from other cookies on the market. But that delicate texture also became its most famous flaw—it breaks way too easily.

The packaging, designed to hold the biscuits snugly, has long been a source of frustration. People often joke about how hard it is to open one without it crumbling in their hands.

Crown has slightly widened the design over the years to reduce breakage, but the change wasn't drastic—and for many, the fragility feels like part of the experience.

At this point, it's practically part of the brand's identity. In fact, its delicate nature has even made its way into Korean internet slang. The phrase "Couque D'asse Mental" (쿠크다스 멘탈) is now used to describe someone who gets easily discouraged or emotionally shaken—just like the cookie that crumbles at the lightest touch.

Online comic joking about 'Couque D'asse Mental'

People may poke fun at how fragile it is, but *Couque D'asse* remains one of Korea's most beloved biscuits. If you enjoy subtly sweet, buttery snacks that pair perfectly with coffee or tea, this one's a must-try.

Poka-Chips 포카칩

Korea's Potato Chip King

Technically speaking, *Poka-Chips* wasn't Korea's first potato chip. That title goes to Nongshim's *Potato Chips*, which hit the market in 1980 and enjoyed a monopoly for years. But in 1988, Orion entered the scene with *Poka-Chips* Onion Flavor—and completely changed the game.

So what made *Poka-Chips* stand out? Unlike Nongshim's original, which had a standard salty flavor, Orion led with onion right from the start—an unexpected (but brilliant) move that helped them carve out a niche. In fact, the original salted version didn't even launch until 1992, long after the onion version had already taken over the market.

Of course, *Poka-Chips* has faced its fair share of complaints—mostly about the small portion size and high price. It even earned the nickname "nitrogen snack" because of the extra air in the bag.

But here's the thing—no other potato chip has ever truly unseated it. Not even *Lay's*, the global giant, could match *Poka-Chips* in Korea.

The secret? It's all about that ultra-thin, extra-crispy texture. Orion was so committed to getting it right that they opened a potato research lab in Gangwon back in 1987. After years of testing, they developed a special potato variety called *Dubek* made specifically for snacking.

Potato storage facility inside Orion's Potato Research Lab

Keeping the Crown

But even the king of potato chips had to defend its throne. When international brands like *Pringles* entered the Korean market and started gaining traction, Orion couldn't just sit back—they responded with hilarious ad campaigns reinforcing one key message: only the best-quality potatoes become *Poka-Chips*.

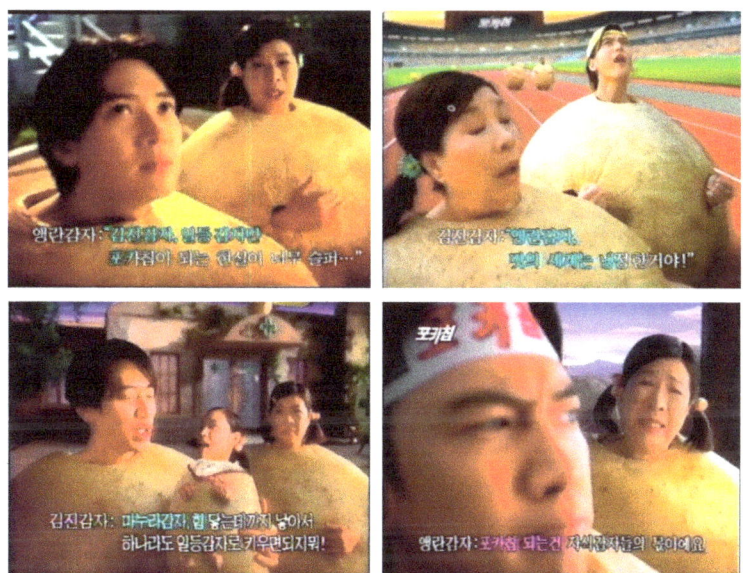

Humorous Poka-Chips ad series from the 1990s

The message was clear: unlike other chips made from processed potato flakes, Poka-Chips are made from real, whole potatoes. The ads were cheeky, a little aggressive—and most importantly, effective.

Thanks to Orion's commitment to quality and clever marketing, Poka-Chips hit a major milestone in 2012, becoming the first Korean potato chip brand to surpass ₩130 billion (approx. $100 million) in annual sales.

And to cement its status as a mega-brand, Orion tackled its biggest criticism—those stingy portions. In 2015, they made a smart move: increasing the portion size by 10% while keeping the price the same. A rare win for snack lovers!

Butter Waffle 버터와플

The Ambition to Stay Timeless

Butter Waffle was created by Crown—the same company behind *Couque D'asse*—in 1997. After striking gold with *Couque D'asse* and its European-style appeal, Crown wanted to take things a step further. This time, they weren't just drawing inspiration—they were aiming for the real deal.

To make it happen, they went straight to the source. Crown imported waffle-making equipment from the Netherlands and, in a bold move for the time, used a generous amount of high-quality European butter and milk to create that ultra-rich, melt-in-your-mouth flavor. But their riskiest decision? Cutting the shelf life down to just three months. In a market where most biscuits lasted a year or more, this was nearly unheard of.

With that level of craftsmanship, Crown positioned *Butter Waffle* as a luxury biscuit. They priced it well above competitors and branded it as "the aristocrat of biscuits." A bit dramatic? Maybe. But it worked. (If you've seen it in North America, you might recognize the tagline *"Nobles Worlds Best Cookies"*—yes, it's over the top and technically not grammatically correct.)

The tagline "The Aristocrat of Biscuits" (과자의 귀족) on Korean packaging

The same tagline used in a TV commercial

To drive home the European vibe, Crown launched a 1997 TV commercial featuring *Butter Waffle* being served to a queen. Adding to the charm, the interpreter in the ad was a real-life translator for the British royal family. Later, the messaging shifted to focus on *Butter Waffle* as the perfect treat for special moments.

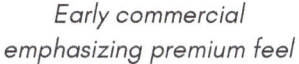

Early commercial emphasizing premium feel

2006 advertisement highlighting Butter Waffle for special occasions

However, not everyone at Crown was convinced. Before the launch, some employees worried the biscuit's firmer texture might turn consumers away. But once it hit store shelves, those concerns quickly faded—*Butter Waffle* took off.

Fast forward to today, and it's still going strong. While other brands constantly roll out new flavors to attract younger consumers, *Butter Waffle* has stayed true to its original recipe. Even the packaging has barely changed. Crown seems committed to keeping it classic, keeping it timeless—and honestly? It's still working.

Honey Butter Chips 허니버터칩

The Sweet & Salty Craze That Swept Korea

Honey Butter Chips were launched in 2014 by Haitai-Calbee, a joint venture between Korea's Haitai Confectionery and Japan's Calbee.

At the time, Orion and Nongshim dominated Korea's potato chip market, so Haitai teamed up with Calbee to introduce something completely different—a sweet and savory chip, something Korea had never seen before.

Japan's Shiawase (Happy) Butter

Interestingly, Calbee had already released a honey butter-flavored chip in Japan back in 2012, but it didn't make much of a splash. When *Honey Butter Chips* hit Korean shelves two years later, though, the reaction was entirely different.

At first, the chips gained slow but steady traction through social media word-of-mouth. But then, things snowballed into a full-blown craze. Suddenly, *Honey Butter Chips* were impossible to find. Supermarket shelves were wiped clean, convenience stores were always sold out, and online resellers were charging up to ten times the original price.

A convenience store sign announcing Honey Butter Chips are sold out

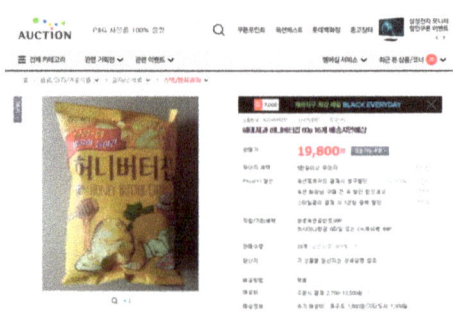

Honey Butter Chips being resold for ten times the price on online auction sites

As the shortage worsened, the frenzy escalated. Korean engineers even built an app to track *Honey Butter Chip* restocks, helping desperate snack lovers locate them in real time. At that point, it wasn't just a snack trend—it was a full-on cultural phenomenon.

The app released in 2014 showing where
Honey Butter Chips were restocked

Of course, the unique sweet-and-salty flavor played a big role in the chip's success. But it was the scarcity that truly drove the obsession. While social media fueled demand, Haitai held off on expanding production—it was too risky in case the craze fizzled. Instead, they ran their existing factories at full capacity, but it still wasn't enough. The constant shortage only made people want them more—a textbook case of supply-and-demand psychology.

Eventually, once Haitai was sure the demand wasn't just a passing fad, they expanded production in 2016 and launched new flavors.

Today, *Honey Butter Chips* are easy to find in Korea and even in international markets. The hype may have faded, but unlike most viral food trends that disappear completely, *Honey Butter Chips* earned a lasting spot in Korea's snack world—proof that sweet and savory chips weren't just a phase. They were here to stay.

Turtle Chips 꼬북칩

The Snack That Broke the Mold

After *Honey Butter Chips* took Korea by storm, there wasn't another major breakout snack for a while. But to be fair, since the 1970s, Korea has seen thousands of snack flavors and textures come and go. With long-standing bestsellers already dominating store shelves, launching a brand-new mega-hit was no easy feat.

Turtle Chips was Orion's ambitious attempt to shake things up and claim a spot among Korea's top snacks. While they never officially confirmed it, many believe the snack was inspired by *Aerial*—a four-layered, ultra-crispy Japanese chip that debuted in 2009.

Orion spent years trying to replicate that signature multi-layered crunch. But when they couldn't quite get it right, they paused development. Instead of rushing it, they doubled down—investing ₩10 billion (about $7.5 million) and several more years into research and production. Finally, in 2017, the long-awaited *Turtle Chips* came out.

Because it introduced a totally new texture and shape, *Turtle Chips* immediately clicked with Korean consumers. That one-of-a-kind crunch—like eating several chips at once—was unlike anything else on the market. Social media buzz pushed its popularity even further, eventually leading to a supply shortage. And of course, that only made people want it more.

With demand soaring, Orion quickly expanded the lineup with new flavors. Over the next year, they rolled out Cinnamon, Shrimp, and Himalayan Salt, but none made much of an impact. Then in 2020, they struck gold with *Choco Churros*.

The sweet, chocolatey flavor was an instant hit—and as demand surged, even the original *Corn Soup* flavor saw a major resurgence. By December 2020, *Turtle Chips* officially joined Orion's top three best-selling snacks—alongside *Choco Pie* and *Poka-Chips*.

Global Market, Local Tastes

From the start, Orion had its sights set on the global market. But instead of simply exporting the same flavors, they focused on tailoring them to local preferences.

In the U.S., for example, Orion specifically targeted the Hispanic market—known for its love of bold, spicy flavors—by launching Flaming Lime. It quickly became a strong seller, driving a significant portion of U.S. sales. Encouraged by its success,  Orion followed up with locally inspired flavors like Truffle Salt and Sweet Vanilla, helping Turtle Chips gain even more traction in North America.

Building on that momentum, Orion fine-tuned its strategy for other regions too—especially in India and Vietnam. They established local production and developed region-specific flavors, making a full-scale push into both countries.

Turtle Chips in Vietnam with its Korean name "Masita,"
meaning "delicious" in Korean

So next time you're browsing your local snack aisle, keep an eye out—you might just spot a *Turtle Chips* flavor made especially for your region!

Part 3

Frozen Treats

weet, Cold, and
Uniquely Korean

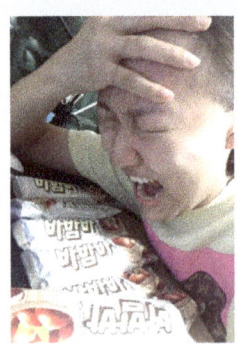

Bravo Cone 부라보콘

The Ice Cream That Made History

In 1970, *Bravo Cone* became Korea's first-ever cone ice cream. Up until the 1960s, the only options were popsicles and soft-serve. And if you wanted soft-serve, you had to track down a street vendor with a cart—which wasn't even that easy in most places.

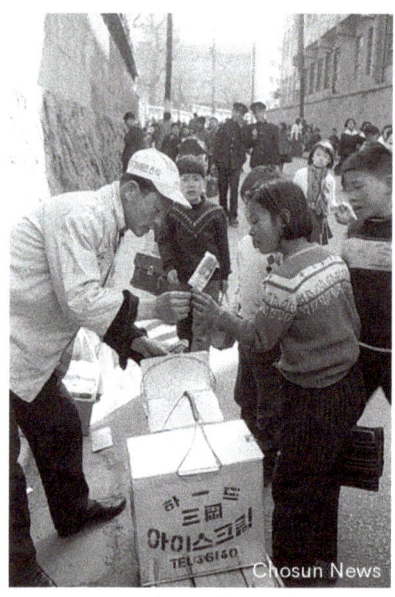

Street vendor selling soft-serve ice cream in the 1960s

That all started to change in 1968, when Haitai brought in production equipment from Denmark and introduced modern ice cream-making technology to Korea. But even with the right machines, producing ice cream locally wasn't simple. One major hurdle was sourcing skim milk powder—a key ingredient. Since it was hard to find in Korea at the time, Haitai obtained it from the U.S. military.

As for toppings, pricier imported options like almonds were out of reach, so they went with something more accessible: peanuts—a familiar and affordable choice for Korean consumers.

However, the biggest challenge wasn't the ingredients—it was the cone itself. How do you keep it crunchy without it getting soggy? Haitai's solution was to coat the inside with chocolate.

But chocolate-making technology was still limited, and the coating often melted and pooled at the bottom of the cone along with the ice cream.

That accident turned out to be a genius stroke. By the time people reached the bottom, they found a surprise chunk of chocolate waiting— and they loved it.

So even though it wasn't perfect, *Bravo Cone* launched with Korea's best ice cream tech at the time. Media outlets rushed to cover the debut, and demand exploded.

Wholesale buyers flooded the factory with orders, and the chaos got so intense that Haitai had to block the factory entrance just to keep things under control.

The launch of Bravo Cone in 1970

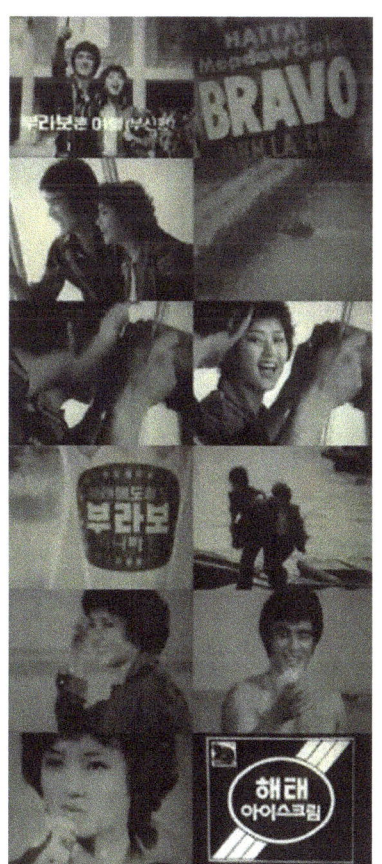

A Nationwide Sensation

Riding the wave of success, Haitai went all in on marketing. They brought in top celebrities for TV and magazine ads, pairing them with a catchy jingle:

"Let's meet at 12, Bravo Cone.
Let's meet together, Bravo Cone.
A sweet little date, Haitai Bravo Cone."

Over the decades, that same tune was reused by a string of A-list celebrities, turning it into an unforgettable earworm for generations.

Going Retro to Win Back Young Consumers

For millennials and older generations, Bravo Cone is packed with nostalgia. But for younger consumers—those born after 2000—the emotional connection wasn't there. Haitai tried to stay relevant by modernizing the packaging and introducing premium flavors, but in doing so, they lost some of the snack's original charm.

So in 2021, Haitai made a bold move: they brought back the original 1970s packaging. The retro design stood out in a sea of sleek, premium-looking brands.

Younger consumers took notice—many even looked up the brand's history and began appreciating its legacy.

Knowing the power of smart marketing, Haitai went one step further. They retired the old-school jingle and brought in actor Lee Byung-hun for a new commercial. Instead of leaning on nostalgia, the ad reimagined *Bravo Cone* with a punchy, action-movie twist on the classic "Let's meet at 12" line.

2021 TV ad featuring Lee Byung-hun

Thanks to the clever rebrand, *Bravo Cone* reclaimed its title as Korea's #1 cone ice cream—a spot it had previously lost to its longtime rival, World Cone. But now that World Cone has taken the lead again, one big question remains: Can *Bravo Cone* keep winning over new generations—while staying true to its roots?

Together 투게더

The Ice Cream That Brought Families Together

First introduced in 1974, *Together* was Korea's first premium ice cream made with fresh milk. It quickly became the signature ice cream of Binggrae, one of the country's largest dairy companies. The name *Together* was chosen through an internal contest, reflecting the brand's vision: an ice cream meant to be shared with family and friends.

At the time, *Together* was considered a luxury—it cost as much as 60 regular ice pops. So Binggrae positioned it as a special treat for families to enjoy during happy moments. It soon earned a nickname: payday ice cream—the one dad would bring home after getting his paycheck.

1980s Together ad. The main tagline reads: "Daddy is the best." (우리아빠 최고)

Reflecting that image, most ads in the 1980s featured fathers coming home from work with a tub of *Together*, set to the catchy jingle: *"Mom and Dad, together—together, together!"*

For many Koreans who grew up in the '70s and '80s, *Together* brings back warm memories of family and childhood.

Keeping Up with the Times

For decades, *Together* stayed true to its family-first image, anchored by its signature 30oz golden tub of vanilla ice cream. But even timeless classics have to evolve.

Korean society has changed dramatically—especially with the world's lowest birth rate. Between 1985 and 2005, four-person households were the norm.

By 2010, two-person households had taken the lead. But by 2015, one-person households made up over 27% of all households, becoming the most common household type.

With fewer large families, it became harder to sell ice cream based purely on nostalgia and tradition. So *Together* adapted. Instead of relying solely on its "family" image, the brand introduced new flavors like chocolate, strawberry, and black sesame to appeal to younger consumers. It also launched a *Miniature* version (about one-third the original size), followed by *Together Signature* (even smaller), catering to single-person households and on-the-go snacking.

Signature

Miniature

Original

Beyond size and flavor, the brand also redefined its message. No longer just about family, *Together* now promotes a broader sense of connection and shared joy. The shift is clear when you compare past and present ads.

1988 ad highlighting family's special moments

2021 ad celebrating Korean Independence and social giving

For nearly half a century, *Together* has been a symbol of family ice cream. Now, it's evolving with the times. What it becomes for the next generation —well, that story's still being written.

Korea's Rapidly Changing Population and Its Impact on the Snack Industry

By now, most people know that South Korea has the lowest birth rate in the world. In 2024, it rose slightly to 0.75—the first uptick in nine years—but the under-20 population continues to shrink at a record pace.

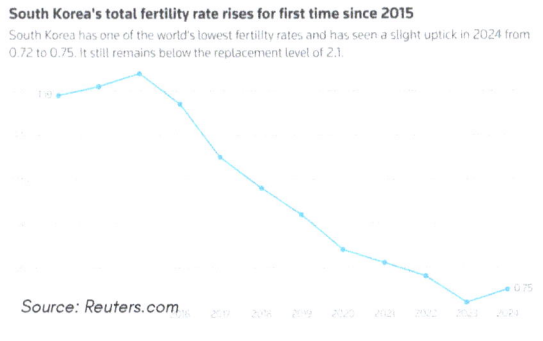

South Korea's total fertility rate rises for first time since 2015
South Korea has one of the world's lowest fertility rates and has seen a slight uptick in 2024 from 0.72 to 0.75. It still remains below the replacement level of 2.1.

Source: Reuters.com

Naturally, this demographic shift is reshaping daily life—including how people eat. Walk through any Korean supermarket today, and you'll see more single-serving meals, portion-sized snacks, and even cookware designed for one.

This trend is also reshaping how Korean food companies grow. With fewer kids and teens at home, snack and ice cream brands—many of which traditionally focused on younger consumers—are now turning their attention to overseas markets where youth populations are booming.

So now, countries like India, Vietnam, and Brazil have become especially attractive, and Korean brands are going after them with bold investments and ambitious plans.

Korean snack brands focusing on key markets like India, Vietnam, and Brazil

Nougat Bar 누가바

The Quiet Game Changer

Back in the early 1970s, most frozen snacks in Korea were simple, water-based pops made with flavored syrup and sugar. These were commonly called "hard" (하드) ice cream—a term borrowed from English, even though they weren't technically ice cream. Walk into any supermarket or street stall, and nearly every frozen treat fell into this "hard" ice pop category.

Then came *Nougat Bar*, quietly changing the game. Instead of a frozen, syrupy core, it featured creamy vanilla ice cream wrapped in a thin layer of nougat chocolate. It was Korea's first stick ice cream with a chocolate coating—and people loved it.

1970s Nougat Bar ad—Haitai explaining why Nougat Bar and Bravo Cone were priced higher than other products.

Unlike typical ice pops, *Nougat Bar*'s soft, creamy texture made it a hit not just with kids, but also with adults. Over time, as more chocolate-coated, soft-textured stick ice creams entered the market, *Nougat Bar* gradually became more popular among middle-aged and older consumers.

And yet, it has never fallen out of Korea's Top 10 best-selling ice creams. It continues to quietly hold its ground—thanks to decades of loyal fans who keep coming back for that nostalgic, simple, and timeless taste.

B.B.Big 비비빅

From Old-School Hit to Cool

B.B.Big first appeared in 1975, bringing something totally different to Korea's ice cream scene—a firm, stick-style bar filled with sweet red bean paste. From the beginning, it wasn't exactly a kid's favorite. With its dense texture and subtly sweet flavor, it naturally appealed more to middle-aged and older consumers.

But here's the funny thing: a lot of people who grew up in the '70s and '80s remember hating *B.B.Big* as kids—only to find themselves loving it as adults.

And the brand knows this well. While other ice creams chased trends with creamier, sweeter flavors, *B.B.Big* leaned into its reputation as a grown-up treat. It introduced new flavors inspired by traditional Korean ingredients that older generations love: injeolmi (roasted soybean powder), black sesame, pumpkin, and more.

B.B.Big Black Sesame Flavor

As it turns out, the timing was perfect. In recent years, millennials and Gen Z have embraced everything retro and nostalgic, fueling the rise of the "Halmaenial" trend—a mashup of *halmoni* (Korean for grandma) and millennial. By 2024, "granny marketing" was in full swing—not just in food but across fashion, design, and branding. What once felt outdated is now quirky, cool, and hipster-approved.

With clever marketing and nostalgic-but-fresh new flavors, *B.B.Big* has become one of Korea's top-selling bar ice creams—proving that some legends only get better with time.

Various brands featuring grandma celebrities

Babamba 바밤바

Owning the "Ajae" Taste

Among Korea's longest-running stick ice creams, *Babamba* has been around since 1976—sticking proudly to its chestnut flavor. The name is just as straightforward: *bam* (Korean for chestnut) + bar, with an extra *ba* at the front to make it catchier.

For years, *Babamba* carried a "mom and dad" reputation. In Korea, if you say you love *Babamba*, *Nougat Bar*, or *B.B.Big*, someone might tease you for having *ajae* taste—*ajae* being short for *ahjussi* (아저씨), or middle-aged man.

But instead of trying to shake that image, *Babamba* leaned in. Rather than chasing trends, it embraced its *ajae* identity—rolling out witty, self-aware ads that proudly positioned *Babamba* as the ultimate grown-up ice cream. And somehow, Gen Z got on board.

Viral meme about parents always buying Babamba

Then came actor Park Sung-woong, a longtime Babamba fan, who casually made up a three-line acrostic poem featuring the brand — complete with a classic ajae-style pun. The bit was originally cut from broadcast (since it mentioned real brand names), but two years later, the clip resurfaced on YouTube — and went viral.

YouTube Channel, Knowingbros 아는형님

Haetae saw the perfect opportunity. They made him the official model for *Babamba* and *Simona*, another of their ice cream brands. The ad was a hit. Eventually, they even released *Simona Babamba*—a mashup of the two.

The viral Babamba ad with Ajae-style humor

Simona Babamba, a combination of Simona and Babamba

Gen Z loved it. They connected with the backstory, the self-aware humor, and the way *Babamba* proudly stayed true to itself. Instead of rebranding for younger audiences, it doubled down on its old-school charm—and that's exactly what made it cool again.

With loyal middle-aged fans on one side and younger generations embracing the irony on the other, *Babamba* isn't going anywhere anytime soon.

Dweji Bar 돼지바

The Genius of Fun Marketing

Dweji Bar is a crispy, chocolate biscuit-coated ice cream bar filled with vanilla ice cream and strawberry syrup.
In North America, it's sold as the *Crispy Crunch Ice Bar*—but in Korea, it proudly keeps its original name: *Dweji Bar* (돼지바), which literally means "Piggy Bar."

Why the name change overseas? Well, calling something a *"Piggy Bar"* in English might not go over so well—culturally, socially, and even religiously. But here's the funny part—even in Korea, the name raised eyebrows at first.

Back in 1983, when *Dweji Bar* was created, it happened to be the Year of the Pig (according to the Chinese Zodiac). The president of Lotte Foods at the time believed naming the ice cream after the pig would symbolize prosperity and good fortune. Not everyone agreed—because, let's face it, *"Piggy Bar"* isn't the most appetizing name. But he stuck with it, and as it turns out, he was right—it became a massive hit from day one.

These days, *Dweji Bar* is known for its genius viral marketing. Instead of playing it safe, the brand leans into the absurd, weird, and unexpected—the kind of stuff that gets people talking online. They've even run idea contests, asking consumers to come up with wild flavor concepts like:

Kimchi Flavor   *Bacon Milkshake Flavor*   *Wasabi Flavor*   *Cucumber Flavor*

None of these flavors ever made it to stores—but that wasn't the point. *Dweji Bar* figured out how to create buzz without big ad spend, while also learning what people actually wanted. A few crowd-sourced ideas even became real products, like the *Dweji Bar Sandwich* and *Dweji Bar Hot Dog*.

Dweji Bar Sandwich   *Dweji Bar Hot Dog*

These quirky creations sparked curiosity—and once people tried them, they couldn't help but post their reactions. That turned into free, viral marketing. For Lotte, it was a total jackpot.

So, what do you think? Would you try these—or do they sound totally inedible?

World Cone 월드콘

The King of Ice Cream in Korea

For over a decade, *Bravo Cone* ruled Korea's ice cream market without serious competition. But in 1986, Lotte's *World Cone* arrived—and it didn't take long to shake things up.

Lotte created *World Cone* with a daring goal: to make the most memorable and best-loved ice cream cone—not just in Korea, but around the world. True to its name, they went bigger and took a more ambitious approach, launching a premium strategy that set it apart from the rest.

Lotte's aggressive approach paid off. Just two years after its debut, *World Cone* overtook *Bravo Cone* as Korea's #1-selling cone. By 1996, it had claimed the top spot in the entire Korean ice cream market—a position it held for decades.

1986 ad with the biggest teen stars of the time

But size alone wasn't what made *World Cone* a success. It was a game-changer in quality. Unlike *Bravo Cone* and other competitors at the time, *World Cone* had a higher dairy fat content for a richer, creamier texture. On top of that, it featured eye-catching toppings that made it instantly more appealing.

Lotte even took inspiration from *Bravo Cone*. Recognizing the popularity of its chocolate-filled tip, they added a clever twist: a plastic base at the bottom of the cone filled with an extra-thick chunk of chocolate.

This detail gave the cone a satisfying texture contrast—and for many fans, it became the best part. Eventually, improvements in production made the plastic base unnecessary, but some nostalgic fans still miss the gooey, ice-cream-soaked chocolate that used to collect inside it.

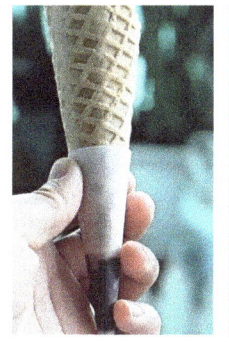

Of course, great taste alone wasn't enough. Lotte knew a product had to stand out before anyone took a bite. From the start, *World Cone* popped off store shelves with its striking red packaging—instantly giving it a premium, exciting vibe.

Soft ice cream packaging in the 1980s vs. World Cone's design positioned as a premium product

Now, as Korea's reigning ice cream king, *World Cone* isn't letting go of its crown anytime soon. Lotte has doubled down on its "World-Class Ice Cream" identity, featuring global celebrities in new marketing campaigns under the "WorlCle" (월클, short for "World Class") slogan.

Top Volleyball player Kim Yeon-koung

Top eSports Player Faker

Samanco 붕어싸만코

Korea's Ultimate Comfort Ice Cream

Samanco is the ice cream version of *Bungeo-ppang*—
a typical winter street snack in Korea: a warm, fish-shaped
pastry filled with sweet red bean paste. The name comes from *bungeo*
(crucian carp, a type of fish) and *ppang* (bread)—but don't worry, there's
no fish involved!

Bungeo-ppang

Bungeo (crucian carp)

Bungeo-ppang actually originated from Japan's *Taiyaki* (たい焼き), which means "baked snapper." The snack made its way to Korea in the 1930s during the Japanese occupation. In Japan, snapper is a commonly eaten fish, but in Korea, it wasn't well known—so locals swapped the name for bungeo, a fish Koreans were more familiar with.

By the 1950s, with the U.S. exporting flour to Korea in large quantities, *bungeo-ppang* became even more popular as a comforting winter snack.

A fun cultural note: In Korea, when someone looks just like their parent, people often say they're *"Mommy's bungeo-ppang"* or *"Daddy's bungeo-ppang"*—because, like the snack, it's as if they came from the exact same mold.

With *bungeo-ppang* so deeply rooted in Korean culture, it was only a matter of time before someone turned it into a frozen treat. Unsurprisingly, Japan led the way—releasing *"Taiyaki Ice"* in 1986, which quickly became a hit.

Four years later, in 1990, Binggrae launched its own version in Korea: *Samanco*. But just as things were taking off, traces of heavy metals were found in red beans imported from China. This led to a ban—and *Samanco*'s production came to a halt.

Luckily, by 1991, Korea had joined the Uruguay Round trade agreement, which lowered tariffs and allowed Binggrae to begin sourcing red beans from South America. With new ingredients in hand, *Samanco* made its return.

Naturally, fans of *bungeo-ppang* were eager to try the ice cream version. The moment it returned to shelves, *Samanco* became a must-try—and for decades, it's remained one of Korea's best-selling ice creams.

Original Samanco packaging at launch and
its design evolution over the years

Today, you'll find *Samanco* in flavors like *tteok* (rice cake), chocolate, walnut, and custard. But if any flavor gives the original a run for its money, it's the sweet and creamy custard version.

These days, fans are split into two camps: Team Original vs. Team Custard.

Which one would you try first—red bean or custard?

Melona 메로나

The Ice Cream That Turned It All Around

Merona is a melon-flavored stick ice cream
that Binggrae launched in 1992—and believe it or not, it helped rescue the company during a financial crisis. After the massive success of *Together Ice Cream* in 1974, Binggrae had expanded into ramen and bakery businesses. But growing too quickly stretched the company thin and strained its finances.

That's when one employee, inspired by a trip to Southeast Asia, pitched an idea: a melon-flavored ice cream. There was just one problem—at the time, melons like honeydew and cantaloupe were considered luxury fruits in Korea. They were expensive, hard to find, and unfamiliar to most Koreans. Even the research team had no idea what a "real" melon was supposed to taste like.

They bought up whatever they could find at high-end department stores, but the melons had spent too long in transit. By the time they were tested, they'd lost their flavor—leaving a dull, slightly bitter impression. Clearly, this wasn't going to work.

So, the team got creative. Instead of relying solely on imported melons, they took inspiration from a local summer favorite: chamoe (참외), Korea's yellow melon. While it didn't taste exactly like honeydew or cantaloupe, chamoe had a similar gentle sweetness and light fragrance. After plenty of trial and error, they landed on a hybrid flavor—somewhere between chamoe and Western melon. And just like that, *Merona* was born.

Chamoe (참외)

When it launched, *Merona* felt like a luxury. It gave everyday consumers a taste of what seemed like a fancy, foreign fruit—without the price tag. And it wasn't just the flavor that stood out. *Merona*'s soft, chewy texture was totally different from anything else on the market at the time, making it feel refreshing and new.

A 1990s ad targeting Gen X in their 20s

The response was huge. *Merona* didn't just sell well—it helped Binggrae bounce back from its financial troubles, turning losses into profits and even overtaking *Bravo Cone* as the top-selling ice cream in Korea for a while.

Merona's Standout Marketing Moves

Merona might already be one of Korea's top ice cream brands—both at home and abroad—but staying on top is a different challenge.

To keep things fresh, *Merona* has launched some playful, out-of-the-box collaborations that extend far beyond the freezer aisle.

Merona X fashion brand Fila *Merona X soju (rice wine) brand Chamisul* *Merona X bakery brand Tous les Jours*

These crossovers have scored major points with younger consumers— showing how even the most familiar brand can evolve and stay relevant.

Seolleim 설레임

The Premium Freezie for Grown-Ups

In Korean, *Seolleim* (설레임) describes that fluttery, heart-skipping feeling you get when you're excited or a little nervous. But the name has a second, more poetic layer: it's made up of Chinese characters—*snow* (雪), *to come* (來), and *to drip* (淋)—pronounced the Korean way. Together, they evoke the image of "falling like snow"—soft, delicate, and melt-in-your-mouth delicious. For international markets, Lotte went with the name *Snow Ice Milkshake*.

In the early 2000s, Korean kids were obsessed with freezies—those colorful frozen tubes you tear open with your teeth. But let's be honest, they weren't exactly the kind of thing adults felt cool carrying around.

So Lotte thought: What if they made a more elevated version of a freezie —something adults could enjoy too? The result was *Seolleim*: a slushy-style ice cream in a sleek pouch that felt premium, easy to carry, and fun to eat. At the time, nothing like it existed on the Korean market.

When it launched in 2003, *Seolleim* came in just two flavors: coffee and mixed fruit. But the response was immediate—it made a splash right away, with no real rivals in sight.

The following year, Lotte introduced a new flavor: milkshake. And that's when things really took off. The milkshake version became such a sensation that, in 2005, it even beat the long-standing ice cream king: *World Cone*. Today, the milkshake flavor accounts for a whopping 75% of *Seolleim*'s total sales.

2003 lineups

2005 lineups

2022 lineups

Seolleim's 2022 ad campaign—spotlighting its biggest fans:
women in their 20s and 30s

The Viral Hack

No one really knows who started it, but somewhere along the way, Korean social media stumbled onto a snack combo that just works: *Seolleim Milkshake + red bean bun.*

Here's how to try it: knead the *Seolleim* pouch with your hands until it turns into a smooth, slushy texture. Then grab a *danpatppang* (단팥빵, red bean bun—you'll find it at most Asian bakeries or supermarkets) and squeeze that creamy goodness right into the center.

Red bean
bun

It's a mashup of creamy and chewy, rich and just sweet enough. The mellow milkiness of *Seolleim* pairs perfectly with the gentle sweetness of red bean paste.

Part 4.

Drinks

Cool, Refreshing,
and a Daily Pick-Me-Up

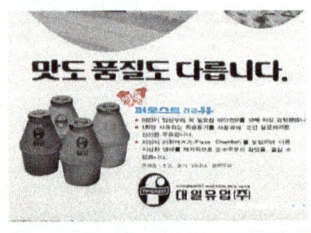

Chilsung Cider 칠성 사이다
Korea's Biggest Threat to Coca-Cola

Chilsung Cider is one of Korea's most iconic drinks—second only to Coca-Cola in sales. Despite the name, though, it's not actually cider. Taste-wise, it's closer to *Sprite* or *7UP*. So when Koreans order 'cider' abroad and get handed apple cider instead, it's always a bit of a surprise. In Korea, *saida* (사이다, cider) refers to a clear, lemon-lime soda—and most of the time, that means *Chilsung Cider*.

This style of "cider" actually traces back to Japan. In the late 1800s, "champagne cider"—a fizzy apple-flavored soda—was popular among Japan's upper class. By the early 1900s, it had made its way to Korea, introduced by Japanese merchants.

Source: Incheon City

1905 Japanese "Champagne Cider" ad from the Gyeongin Railway in Korea.

Then in 1949, seven Korean entrepreneurs teamed up to create a homegrown version using domestic technology. They named their brand Chilsung—first to represent the "seven surnames" of the founders, and later reinterpreted as "seven stars," symbolizing longevity and success.

With big ambitions, they launched *Chilsung Cider* in May 1950. But just a

month later, the Korean War broke out. The company's factory was nearly destroyed, left with only its bare frame. Still, they didn't give up. With new investors and relentless effort, the team rebuilt—and refined what would become Chilsung's signature: a clean, crisp, no-frills refreshment.

As postwar Korea recovered, the thirst for soft drinks exploded. Chilsung Cider grew quickly, but for a while, it was still seen as a special-occasion treat.

To reach everyday consumers, Chilsung ramped up its marketing. They launched a catchy jingle performed by pop star Hye Eun-yee—and soon, everyone was humming along.

1976 ad featuring the famous jingle

By the 1980s, Chilsung leaned into a "clean and pure" image—something that set it apart from global soda brands packed with caffeine, food coloring, and artificial ingredients. Chilsung proudly positioned itself as the better-for-you choice, promoting its "3 NOs": no color, no caffeine, no artificial flavors.

From Soda to Slang: The "Cider" Effect

These days, *saida* means more than just soda—it's become a full-on cultural expression in Korea. When someone says exactly what everyone's been thinking— or does something refreshingly honest— people say:

A meme of a "saida moment"

- *"That was total cider."* (As in: totally satisfying.)
- *"What she said? Pure cider."* (Translation: bold, honest, and long overdue.)

Just like that fizzy kick to the throat, *saida* moments are all about clearing the air and hitting reset.

Bacchus 박카스

The Energy Drink Koreans Can't Live Without

You can't talk about Korea's beverage scene without mentioning *Bacchus*. It was the country's very first energy drink—and arguably, still the most beloved.

In the early 1960s, Korea was still recovering from war, and public health was in rough shape. Most people were working six or seven days a week to help rebuild the nation—and the drink-heavy business culture didn't help.

That's when Kang Shin-ho, founder of Dong-A Pharmaceutical, stepped in with a clear mission: create something that could help people power through exhaustion. The name *Bacchus* comes from the Roman god of wine and festivity—a fitting reference for a drink designed to revive your energy and lift your spirits.

Surprisingly, *Bacchus* didn't begin as a drink. It started out as a pill—but the tablets melted too easily. Then came liquid ampoules, but those shattered in transit. Finally, in 1963, the company landed on the now-iconic brown glass bottle—and that version stuck.

1961-1963 Bacchus evolution

At the time, most Koreans didn't even know what an energy drink was. *Bacchus* barely made a splash—until its bold slogan, "Drink your vitality," started catching attention. Curiosity grew, people tried it, and word spread fast. Just like that, Korea's energy drink era was underway.

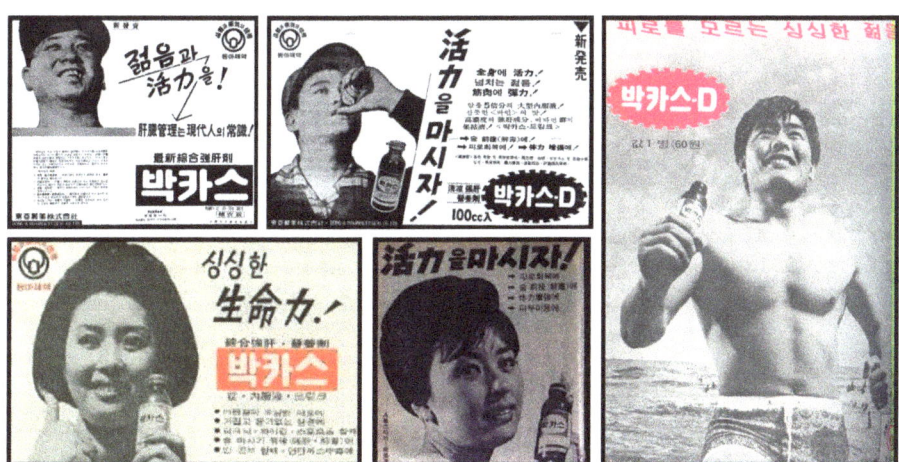

1960s Bacchus newspaper ads focused on 'youth' and 'vitality'

Once *Bacchus* claimed the top spot, it shifted its message. It wasn't just about energy anymore—it was about resilience and showing up for life. Ads began featuring students, office workers, and parents pushing through tough days: "Shake off today's fatigue today."

That message resonated in a country sprinting through rapid economic growth. People felt seen—and they loved it.

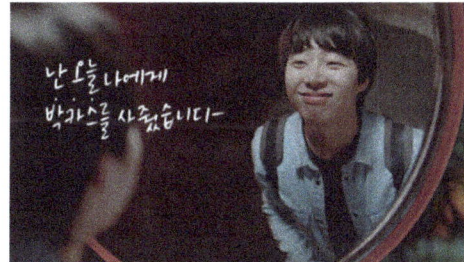

Bacchus ads capturing exhaustion, resilience, and fresh starts

Over time, *Bacchus* became more than just a drink. It became a spirit. A bottle of *Bacchus* meant: *life gets hard, but we keep going.* Its ads didn't just sell a product—they captured a national mindset.

Bacchus Goes Southeast

Like many Korean brands, *Bacchus* began eyeing international markets in the 1980s. But its most unexpected success story? Southeast Asia—especially Cambodia.

When *Bacchus* entered the Cambodian market in 2009, sales took off—growing over 100% year after year. And by 2011, it pulled off the unthinkable: dethroning *Red Bull* to become the No.1 energy drink in the country.

Bacchus outdoor ad in Phnom Penh

Today, *Bacchus* is going all-in on Southeast Asia—on the hunt for its next "Cambodia" in fast-growing markets like Vietnam and the Philippines.

Bacchus ad in Vietnam starring the famous Korean coach of the national football team

Dong-A Pharma Philippines CEO Amen Say (second from left) showing support at a local E-sports event

Will Korea's decades-old playbook work again? No one knows for sure. But with *Bacchus*'s track record—and its uncanny knack for striking the right chord in marketing—it's hard to bet against it.

Banana Flavored Milk 바나나맛 우유

Korea's Sweetest Throwback

Banana milk was born in the 1970s, when the Korean government was actively promoting dairy consumption.

National Archives of Korea

Dairy cows imported from various Western countries in 1961

Between 1962 and 1966, Korea's first economic development plan included boosting the dairy industry to build a more sustainable food supply. Cows were imported from the U.S., New Zealand, Australia, Canada, and Germany—and milk production suddenly soared.

The issue was, no one really knew what to do with all that milk. The government pushed people to drink more of it, but milk wasn't something most Koreans were used to—and to make things worse, many are naturally lactose intolerant. For a lot of people, a glass of milk just meant one thing: a stomachache.

So Binggrae (then known as Daeil Dairy) started looking for a smart way to make milk more appealing—and easier to sell. Eventually, they decided on bananas. At the time, bananas were seen as a luxury fruit—so expensive that most people had never even tasted one.

The Farmers' Newspaper

In the 1970s, bananas were 100x the price of bus fare, and 10x the cost of a bowl of noodles.

The team believed that turning it into an affordable, drinkable flavor would spark interest and open the door for more people to enjoy milk. And they were right.

1970s Magazine Ad

Even though *banana milk* was pricier than regular milk, it quickly won people over. For those who had never tasted a real banana, the sweet, fruity flavor felt like a glimpse of something rare and special. Interestingly, it didn't even contain real banana—just banana flavoring and a hint of vanilla. But with its soft sweetness, creamy texture, and bright yellow color, it was unlike anything Koreans had seen before. It felt like a little luxury in a bottle.

And while the taste sealed the deal, there's another reason it's stuck around for nearly five decades: that bottle.

When designing the packaging, Binggrae wanted something that stood out from the standard glass bottles and plastic packs. While brainstorming ideas that felt familiar and meaningful to Koreans, the team stumbled

upon a traditional moon jar at a pottery exhibition—and inspiration struck.

The final shape, inspired by the smooth curves of Korean dal hangari (moon-shaped jars), debuted in 1974 and hasn't changed since. In 2016, it was even registered as a trademark.

Banana Milk's bottle inspiration—Korean traditional moon-shaped pottery

However, in most countries outside of Korea, *banana milk* is exported in sterilized cartons due to shelf life limitations. To preserve the original charm, an image of the iconic bottle is printed right on the packaging.

The Post-Bath Ritual

If you've watched K-dramas, you've probably seen *banana milk* pop up more than once. For many Koreans, it's more than just a drink—it's a comforting taste of childhood.

A scene from the K-drama Go Back Couple—drinking banana milk after a bath

Those born before the 1990s likely remember regular trips to public bathhouses. Sure, most kids weren't exactly thrilled about sitting in a hot, steamy sauna—but they knew what waited for them afterward: *banana milk* and baked eggs.

A typical Korean public bathhouse

Baked eggs (brown and chewy after hours in high heat) and banana milk

Of course, this connection doesn't span every generation. As more families installed bathtubs at home, public bath visits began to decline. After the COVID-19 pandemic, concerns over hygiene and privacy led to an even steeper drop.

Still, for many in the older generations, the public bathhouse remains a space for rest and community—and in that space, *banana milk* continues to be a beloved, nostalgic treat.

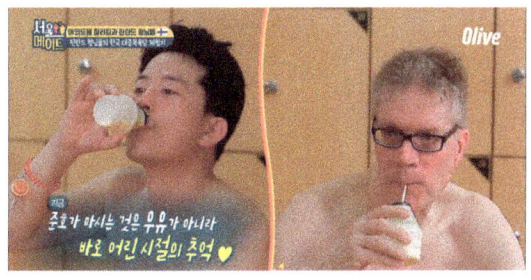

A scene from the TV show Seoul Mate, introducing Korean bathhouses and banana milk

Milkis 밀키스

The Soda That Beat Coke at Its Own Game

Milkis is a carbonated soft drink launched by Lotte Chilsung in 1989. By blending soda with milk, it created a smooth, lightly tangy flavor that quickly became a longtime favorite in Korea.

What most people don't realize is that Coca-Cola actually got there first. Their lookalike product, *Ambasa*, launched in Japan in 1982 and arrived in Korea by 1984—a full five years before *Milkis*.

1980s Ambasa ads—Korea (left) vs. Japan (right)

Lotte modeled *Milkis* after Ambasa but knew they had to find a way to stand out. The two drinks tasted so similar that even in blind tests, people couldn't tell them apart. Clearly, taste alone wasn't going to cut it.

Then came a stroke of luck. A new Korean law had just allowed foreign celebrities to appear in local ads for the first time. Lotte jumped on the opportunity and signed Chow Yun-Fat—one of Asia's biggest stars at the time—as Korea's first-ever foreign commercial model. It was a bold—and expensive—move, but it paid off.

In the commercial, Chow Yun-Fat famously ad-libbed the now-legendary line: "Saranghaeyo (I love you), *Milkis*!" in charmingly awkward Korean. It wasn't scripted—it was completely improvised. But the line became a viral catchphrase and helped catapult *Milkis* into the spotlight.

With the perfect mix of timing, trend, and star power, *Milkis* took off. Today, it's still one of Korea's most beloved soft drinks—recognized by generations and still going strong.

Print ads featuring the viral phrase
"Saranghaeyo, Milkis"

The Viral Hwachae Recipe

Hwachae is a traditional Korean summer punch made with sliced fruits and served ice-cold. The original version uses soda and milk—but Milkis combines both, making it the easiest shortcut to a soft, fizzy twist on hwachae.

Here's how to make it:

1. Cut a watermelon in half, scoop out the flesh, and dice into bite-sized pieces or use a melon baller.
2. Add any fruits you like—grapes, melon, pineapple, or canned fruit cocktail.
3. Pour in chilled *Milkis* and a handful of ice (if you want).

That's it. Sweet, refreshing, and totally addictive—K-style summer in a bowl.

Miero Fiber 미에로 화이바

The Signature Drink for Staying Slim

By the late 1980s, Korea was changing fast. As household incomes rose and Western-style, meat-heavy diets became more common, interest in dieting and wellness started to take off. Just a decade earlier, the country had been grappling with food shortages—so this shift was nothing short of dramatic.

Naturally, brands jumped on the health trend. One of the first to stand out was *Miero Fiber*, a citrusy, orange-flavored fiber drink aimed squarely at women in their 20s and 30s.

The name *Miero Fiber* blends several meanings: *mi* (美), the Chinese character for "beauty"; the Korean postposition -*e*, meaning "toward"; and *ro* (路), meaning "road" or "path." Together, it loosely translates to "*the path to beauty.*"

And the brand fully embraced that message. *Miero Fiber* ads featured the era's top supermodels and rising actresses, promoting the idea that being slim, healthy, and beautiful went hand in hand—with *Miero Fiber* as your daily companion.

*'90s Miero Fiber ads featuring
the top model and actress*

At the time, no other product in Korea was championing this kind of beauty-meets-wellness concept. *Miero Fiber* struck a chord and quickly became a sensation. Within months, a wave of similar fiber drinks flooded the market, all trying to ride the trend.

Decades later, *Miero Fiber*'s core message hasn't changed much. The brand still partners with top celebrities through its *Miero Girls* campaign, spotlighting toned bodies and glowing skin as the aspirational ideal.

Of course, beauty standards vary by culture. While body diversity has gained momentum in places like North America, in Korea, this image of slim, toned beauty continues to resonate—especially among those who admire the aesthetic, even if they support broader body representation.

Miero Girls campaign promoting the "healthy and beautiful" body ideal

After years of success with its original formula, *Miero Fiber* recently launched a zero-sugar version—something many health-conscious consumers had long been waiting for. It still delivers that signature citrus flavor, just with less sweetness.

But *Miero Fiber* isn't alone anymore. These days, zero-sugar, zero-calorie, and "better-for-you" options are everywhere—from snacks and drinks to even ice cream. The brand now faces fierce competition from a new wave of products targeting the same health- and body-conscious audience.

Zero-sugar/calorie products from major beverage brands

Now the question is: how will this decades-strong legacy brand evolve for its next chapter?

Let's Be 레쓰비

Korea's Sweet Spot in a Can

Korea's coffee journey began in the 1890s, but back then, it was a luxury reserved for royals and the upper class. In the early 20th century, coffee began appearing in high-end hotels and tearooms, slowly inching toward the mainstream—but it was still far from accessible for most people.

Dancer Choi Seung-hee having coffee at the Chosun Hotel, 1940s

That changed during and after World War II, when U.S. troops stationed in Korea introduced instant coffee from their military rations. For many Koreans, it was their first taste of coffee.

Even into the 1970s, coffee was still considered a special-occasion drink—something offered to guests rather than enjoyed daily.

But everything shifted in the 1980s, when Korea's first 3-in-1 coffee mix—instant coffee, sugar, and creamer in one stick—was developed. From that point on, coffee started becoming part of everyday life. By the 1990s, cafés were popping up everywhere—and when Starbucks entered Korea, coffee had officially gone mainstream.

Let's Be entered the scene in 1991, just as the coffee boom was heating up. Canned coffee was starting to catch on with younger consumers, thanks in part to the rise of vending machines offering hot or cold drinks year-round. *Let's Be* grew right alongside the trend.

To stand out from other instant coffee brands, *Let's Be* initially marketed itself as drip-brewed from 100% Colombian beans. It was a clever, premium-leaning strategy from the company's point of view—but at the time, most consumers weren't familiar with the reputation of Colombian coffee, and drip-style brewing hadn't really caught on. So the message didn't land as strongly as hoped.

In 1997, Lotte Chilsung hit the reset button. They tweaked the flavor to better suit Korean tastes—adding the now-signature sweet profile—and gave the can a full makeover with its classic blue design.

And they knew exactly who to target: Gen Xers in their 20s, eager for something fresh and different—especially Western-style coffee. So *Let's Be* launched a major ad campaign that dialed up the cool factor.

One ad in particular struck a chord—a young woman checks out the guy in front of her on the bus, then says: "I'm getting off here," implying, "unless you're thinking of getting off with me."

It was cheeky, clever, and instantly memorable. Just like that, *Let's Be* became the coffee of choice for young people. By 1998, it had climbed to the No.1 spot in Korea's canned coffee market.

The legendary ad that won over Korea's Gen X

Since then, *Let's Be* has continued leading the canned coffee scene, expanding its lineup with styles like Americano, Latte, and Hazelnut. More recently, it's embraced global flavors—like Vietnamese coffee and salty-sweet Taiwanese blends.

It's a nod to younger Koreans' evolving tastes, shaped by travel, media, and a thirst for new experiences. *Let's Be* isn't just riding on legacy—it's evolving to stay ahead.

Condition 컨디션

Korea's First Official Hangover Cure

Okay, this might not be something Koreans proudly advertise— but it's no secret: Korea consistently ranks among the top countries for alcohol consumption per person. Drinking is deeply embedded in the culture, whether it's catching up with friends or closing business deals.

New York Times

Dingo Music

Naturally, that kind of drinking culture came with a need: hangover relief. And in the early '90s, *Condition* became the very first drink to offer exactly that.

Before *Condition*, people mostly relied on old-school remedies like honey water or dried pollack soup (buk uh guk)—or they just suffered through it. So when *Condition* hit the market in 1992, no one really knew if people would go for it.

Dried Fish Soup 북어국

But it took off. In its first year, the market was worth only about $1.5 million USD. By the next year, it had jumped to $30 million—and within three years, it had soared over $100 million. *Condition*'s success sparked a flood of similar products in the mid-1990s, as every beverage brand wanted in.

Then came the downturn. Korea's financial crisis in the late '90s hit the alcohol industry hard—and hangover drinks were no exception. Sales plummeted, and many smaller brands disappeared, leaving only a few major players behind.

Today, *Condition* controls nearly 50% of Korea's hangover drink market. Its formula includes 100% Korean-grown oriental raisin tree fruit extract, taurine, niacin, and other ingredients shown to help reduce acetaldehyde—the chemical that causes hangovers—and slow alcohol absorption. No wonder it's a go-to during the end-of-year party season or after a big night out.

Drinking Culture Is Changing – And So Is Condition

Condition may be a household name now, but that doesn't mean it can sit back and relax. Korea's drinking habits are changing—fast.

Younger generations are turning away from the traditional company dinners and multi-round drinking nights (*Hoesik* 회식) that used to stretch late into the evening. These days, people prefer more balanced lifestyles—dinner with friends, a movie, or simply heading home early.

With less drinking overall, there's naturally less demand for hangover cures. And *Condition* is adapting. Rather than positioning itself solely as a "next-morning" fix, *Condition* has started marketing itself as a pre-drinking supplement—something you take before alcohol to help your body recover more easily.

1990s ad targeting heavy-drinking office workers

2025 ad featuring young professionals

As Korea's social culture and demographics continue to shift, it'll be fascinating to watch how *Condition* evolves next—and whether it can remain the top choice in a generation that drinks less but thinks more about wellness.

Birak Shikhye 비락식혜

A Traditional Sweet Reinvented

Sikhye is one of Korea's most beloved traditional drinks—a gently sweet rice punch often served as a dessert after meals. With its mellow flavor and soft grains of rice floating in each sip, it's pure comfort and nostalgia for many Koreans.

Traditional-style Sikhye with floating rice grains

The drink is made by soaking cooked rice in malt water, activating natural enzymes that bring out its subtle sweetness and aroma. It's also rich in dietary fiber and antioxidants, which is why it's long been enjoyed as a digestive aid—especially after big family gatherings like Chuseok (Korean Thanksgiving) or Lunar New Year.

In the early 1990s, when sodas and Western-style fizzy drinks dominated Korea's beverage shelves, *Birak* (the company's name at the time) made a bold move: they turned this traditional homemade dessert drink into a ready-to-drink canned product.

Until then, *sikhye* was something you made at home—usually for special occasions. Suddenly being able to grab it from a vending machine or convenience store anytime, anywhere felt like a quiet revolution.

And the move paid off. By 1995, just two years after its launch, *Birak Sikhye* had sold over 200 million cans—cementing its place as one of the most popular Korean drinks of the decade. Its success even paved the way for other traditional beverages, like *Soo Jeong Gwa* (a cinnamon-ginger punch with dried persimmons), to enter the market.

How to Enjoy Sikhye the Right Way

You can enjoy *sikhye* straight from the fridge—but it hits different when it's lightly frozen to a slushy, ice-cold texture. That's how many Koreans love it, especially after a hot sauna or public bath. In fact, alongside banana milk, it's a staple at *Jjimjilbangs* (Korean-style saunas)—and if banana milk is the kid favorite, *sikhye* is definitely the grown-up go-to.

Sikhye sold in standard plastic bottles —returnable for deposit

Scene from K-drama My Roommate Is a Gumiho showing sikhye and baked eggs in a jjimjilbang

Paldo, the company behind *Birak Sikhye*, knew just how much Koreans loved their *sikhye* ice-cold—especially after sweating it out in the heat. So they teamed up with Dunkin' in Korea to launch limited-time specials like the *Sikhye Ice Crush*, and later, the upgraded *Sikhye Coolatta*—both served with that signature slushy texture.

2018-launched Sikhye Ice Crush

2024-upgraded Sikhye Coolatta

If you want to recreate the experience at home, just pop a can of *sikhye* in the freezer until it starts to freeze around the edges. Give it a good shake before opening to turn it into an instant ice slush. Just be careful when you crack it open—things can get a little wild!

Achimhatsal 아침햇살

The Most Korean and Surprisingly Universal Drink

Let's be honest—*Achimhatsal* isn't the easiest name to pronounce or remember. Depending on where you are, you might see it labeled as *Morning Sunlight*, *Morning Rice Drink*, or *Korean Sweet Rice Drink*. But for this book, we're sticking with the original Korean name: *Achimhatsal*.

The drink debuted in the late '90s, right in the middle of Korea's economic golden era. After more than a decade of diving headfirst into Western food and culture, the mood began to shift. By the late '90s, Koreans were starting to rediscover their own ingredients, flavors, and traditions—with a growing focus on health and national identity.

That's when Woongjin, one of Korea's major food and beverage companies, made a bold move: instead of chasing global drink trends, they went in the opposite direction. They turned to Korea's most foundational ingredient—rice—and created a smooth, subtly sweet roasted rice drink that felt nostalgic, wholesome, and deeply familiar.

At the time, there was nothing else like it. With its creamy texture and toasty, earthy flavor, *Achimhatsal* instantly stood out. It brought in over $30 million in sales in its first year and nearly tripled that the following year—launching a brand-new beverage category in Korea: grain-based drinks. And naturally, it became the category leader.

In 2001, Woongjin featured rising star Song Hye-kyo in a now-famous commercial. In the ad, she's rushing to school after skipping breakfast and drinks a bottle of *Achimhatsal* on the subway — one her mom had given her earlier. The message was clear: : this wasn't just a sweet drink

—it was a simple, healthy way to start your day.

But *Achimhatsal*'s story doesn't end there. In the early 2000s, as Korea began importing more rice from overseas, concerns grew about the future of local farming. Woongjin responded with a clever campaign rooted in national pride: "Support Korean rice. Sometimes, the answer comes from changing your perspective."

They emphasized that *Achimhatsal* was made with 100% Korean-grown rice—framing the drink as more than just nostalgic or nutritious. It became a way to support local farmers and protect Korea's agricultural heritage.

At that point, *Achimhatsal* had evolved from a novelty into something bigger: a symbol of Korean taste, tradition, and homegrown pride.

Woongjin CEO and Song Hye-kyo in an ad encouraging support for domestic rice by drinking Achimhatsal

If you enjoy rice-based drinks or desserts, give *Achimhatsal* a try. Some say it reminds them of *Chè*, the sweet Vietnamese rice dessert—or even *Miki* (ミキ), a traditional fermented rice drink from Okinawa. Add a dash of cinnamon and sugar, and it starts to resemble *Horchata*, the creamy rice drink beloved in Mexico.

Turns out, that smooth, toasty-sweet flavor is more universal than you'd think!

Vita 500 비타500

A New Era in Korea's Energy Aisle

Since the 1960s, Bacchus had ruled Korea's energy drink market with an iron grip. For over 40 years, it reigned as the undisputed No. 1, brushing off wave after wave of challengers.

Kwangdong Pharmaceutical had long been both inspired—and quietly frustrated—by Bacchus's success. But as a company still finding its footing, taking on such a giant head-on felt too risky. So instead of competing on "energy" or "fatigue recovery," they took a different path: targeting younger, health-conscious consumers with a wellness drink packed with 500mg of Vitamin C—well above the recommended daily dose.

They positioned it as a premium health booster, priced it higher than Bacchus, and brought in A-list celebrities to give it a sleek, aspirational edge.

*Early 2000s ad showing Bacchus (left) and Vita 500 (right)
with contrasting brand positions*

And it worked. Before Vita 500, the idea of drinking your vitamins wasn't really a thing. But suddenly, you could grab a bottle of liquid Vitamin C at any convenience store. It felt fresh. It felt healthy. It felt easy.

What really helped Vita 500 take off, though, was the taste. That familiar lemon flavor—what most Koreans associate with the classic "vitamin taste"—was comforting and clean. Compared to Bacchus's stronger, more medicinal flavor, Vita 500 offered a smoother, more refreshing profile that resonated with both men and women across all age groups. And even without caffeine, it still delivered a subtle, feel-good boost.

By 2005, just four years after its debut, Vita 500 pulled off the unthinkable: it briefly overtook Bacchus to become Korea's top-selling energy drink. Bacchus fired back with pointed ads declaring, "The real recovery drink is at the pharmacy." And just like that, a fierce new competition was underway.

Reaching Even Younger Consumers

For years after its launch, Vita 500 zeroed in on a specific audience: high school seniors preparing for Korea's notoriously intense college entrance exam.

These students often study for hours on end, relying on coffee or heavily caffeinated drinks to power through. But Vita 500—with its caffeine-free formula and health-focused image—offered a gentler alternative that parents were much more likely to approve of.

Past Vita 500 campaigns geared toward
college entrance exam season

This smart strategy paid off. Vita 500's exam-season campaigns became an annual tradition—and a clever way to build brand loyalty with future long-term customers. Eventually, even Bacchus took notice of the rising demand for caffeine-free, health-conscious options and launched its own decaf version in 2012 to stay competitive.

That moment made one thing clear: Vita 500 was no longer just the new kid on the block—it had grown into a serious contender for the crown.

University Entrance Exam & What It Means to Korea

Like many countries that developed rapidly in a short time, South Korea is known for its intense culture of competition.

With few natural resources and little to build on after the devastation of war, Korea had one clear path forward: invest in its people. Fueled by grit, discipline, and relentless effort, Koreans studied and worked as if their entire future depended on it—and in many ways, it did. That determination helped transform the country from one of the world's poorest into a proud member of the OECD in just a few decades.

As of 2022, 70% of Koreans aged 25 to 34 hold a postsecondary degree—one of the highest rates in the world. (By comparison, the U.S. sits at around 51%, while the OECD average is about 47%.)

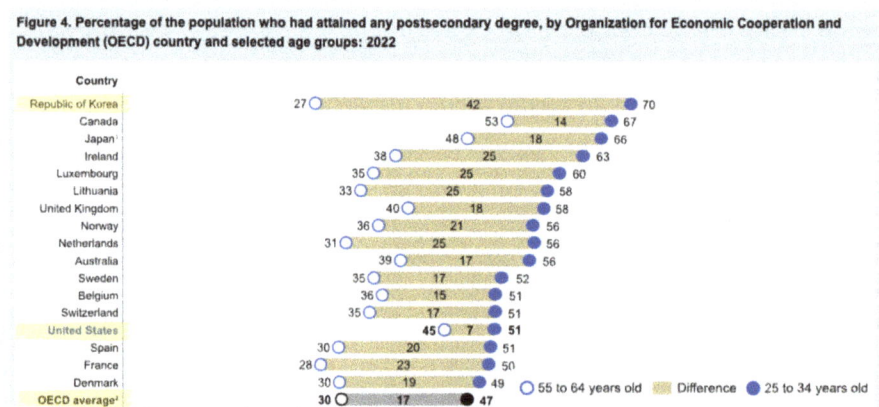

Figure 4. Percentage of the population who had attained any postsecondary degree, by Organization for Economic Cooperation and Development (OECD) country and selected age groups: 2022

National Center for Education Statistics (nces.ed.gov)

But behind that impressive statistic lies a heavy cost. Students in Korea grow up under immense pressure from a young age, all leading up to one high-stakes moment: the university entrance exam. On that day, the entire country slows down—literally.

Yonhap News

Flights are rescheduled. Traffic is redirected to reduce noise near testing sites. Some companies even push back their office hours. All of this—for one exam. But the test is only the beginning. It's the first major hurdle in a long, competitive journey toward securing a job.

Students entering testing sites on exam day

Police escorting a late test-taker through traffic

Planes circling around Incheon and Gimpo Airports during the national English listening exam

Parents praying at a temple

This hyper-competitive environment has faced growing criticism in recent years, especially as Korea struggles with the world's lowest birth rate. Many believe the pressure-cooker education system is one of the key reasons younger generations are delaying marriage—or choosing not to have children at all.

Education, population, and the economy are deeply intertwined—and they shape nearly everything, including how Korean companies plan for the future. It's no coincidence that many of the brands featured in this book are now looking beyond Korea's borders. And honestly, that's probably why you'll be seeing—and enjoying—even more of them around the world soon.

Thank You!

감사합니다

If you've made it this far—thank you.

We didn't just stroll through the snack aisle together. We wandered through Korea's modern history and culture, one bite at a time.

Whether you grew up with these flavors or discovered them for the first time in this book, I hope you felt a sense of connection—to a culture, to a story, or maybe just to a really good bag of chips.

If This Book Made You Smile...

...consider leaving a short review. It helps others discover and enjoy it too—and gives me the chance to keep creating more stories like this!

Amazon Review Link:
https://www.amazon.com/review/create-review?&asin=9781998277957

www.ingramcontent.com/pod-product-compliance
Lightning Source LLC
Chambersburg PA
CBHW051216120626
46547CB00013B/1374

* 9 7 8 1 9 9 8 2 7 7 9 5 7 *